ROAD RACING
FOR
SERIOUS RUNNERS

PETE PFITZINGER
SCOTT DOUGLAS

Human Kinetics

Library of Congress Cataloging-in-Publication Data

Pfitzinger, Peter, 1957-
  Road racing for serious runners / Peter Pfitzinger, Scott Douglas.
    p.   cm.
  Includes bibliographical references (p.).
  ISBN 0-88011-818-0
  1. Running--Training.   2. Running--Physiological aspects.
  I. Douglas, Scott.   II. Title.
  GV1061.5.P45   1998
  796.42--dc21
                                                            98-43137
                                                              CIP
  ISBN-10: 0-88011-818-0
  ISBN-13: 978-0-88011-818-7

Copyright © 1999 by Peter Pfitzinger and Scott Douglas

Acquisitions Editor: Martin Barnard; **Developmental Editor:** C.E. Petit, JD; **Assistant Editor:** Cassandra Mitchell; **Copyeditor:** Bob Replinger; **Proofreader:** Kathy Bennett; **Graphic Designer:** Nancy Rasmus; **Graphic Artists:** Angela K. Snyder and Yvonne Winsor; **Photo Editor:** Boyd LaFoon; **Cover Designer:** Jack Davis; **Photographer (cover):** Victah Sailer; **Printer:** United Graphics

Printed in the United States of America

10   9   8   7   6   5

Human Kinetics
Web site: www.HumanKinetics.com

United States: Human Kinetics
P.O. Box 5076
Champaign, IL 61825-5076
800-747-4457
e-mail: humank@hkusa.com

Canada: Human Kinetics
475 Devonshire Road, Unit 100
Windsor, ON N8Y 2L5
800-465-7301 (in Canada only)
e-mail: orders@hkcanada.com

Europe: Human Kinetics
107 Bradford Road
Stanningley, Leeds LS28 6AT
United Kingdom
+44 (0) 113 255 5665
e-mail: hk@hkeurope.com

Australia: Human Kinetics
57A Price Avenue
Lower Mitcham, South Australia 5062
08 8277 1555
e-mail: liaw@hkaustralia.com

New Zealand: Human Kinetics
Division of Sports Distributors NZ Ltd.
P.O. Box 300 226 Albany
North Shore City, Auckland
0064 9 448 1207
e-mail: info@humankinetics.co.nz

CONTENTS

Foreword by Bill Rodgers   v

Preface   vii

Acknowledgments   ix

PART I   The Physiology of Running

Chapter 1   A Multispeed Approach to Road Racing   3

Chapter 2   Training to Improve $\dot{V}O_2$max
             and Speed   15

Chapter 3   Training to Improve Lactate Threshold
             and Pure Endurance   33

Chapter 4   Optimal Training   51

Chapter 5   Optimal Racing   81

PART II   Training for Peak Performance

Chapter 6   Training to Race 5K   101

Chapter 7   Training to Race 8K to 10K   115

Chapter 8   Training to Race 15K Through Half Marathon   129

Chapter 9   Training for the Marathon   147

Chapter 10   Training to Race Cross-Country   167

Appendix A   183

Appendix B   184

References   187

About the Authors   189

Foreword

The most clearly written and detailed source of information on how to train smart that I've ever read, *Road Racing for Serious Runners* contains the methods by which anyone can improve his or her running and racing. In recent years, I've noticed the quality of information relating to distance-running training has improved dramatically. One of the key exercise physiologists leading the way is Pete Pfitzinger, who practiced what he preaches. Pete made two U.S. Olympic teams in the marathon, and I believe he did so by defeating more "talented" runners who may not have trained or raced as intelligently as Pete did.

Over the last few years I've enjoyed reading Pete's column in *Running Times* magazine. If you've missed those, you now have the opportunity to see what he has to say in this cutting-edge runner's training resource book. I know that Pete did what he advocates in this book, because he was not a regular on the road-racing circuit, but was more like Frank Shorter, Lasse Viren, Grete Waitz, Joan Benoit Samuelson, or Uta Pippig—a runner who aims for a specific goal race.

I recall defeating Pete, as did my friend 1983 Boston Marathon champion Greg Meyer, in the April 1984 Trevira Twosome 10-mile race in New York City. But Pete was lying low. He didn't aim for that race; he was aiming for the U.S. Olympic Marathon Trials race the next month, where he finished first, ahead of not only Greg and me but also Alberto Salazar, then one of the top 10K and marathon men in the world.

As for Pete's coauthor, Scott Douglas, I feel no writer in our sport can write so clearly. This is apparent in *Road Racing for Serious Runners*. Although there is a lot of material, Scott's style of writing allows the reader to absorb the information with ease. Scott has a fine sense of humor and can approach scientific research and our so-serious sport with a wild or humorous comment that makes this significant information read smoothly. This is not a boring book or a book filled with fluff. Some of the topics covered are the importance of carbohydrate loading, peaking and tapering before races, the crucial function of your warm-up and cool-down, and the smart way to do long training runs for the marathon, plus detailed analyses of what you need to do to run faster at every distance from 5K to the marathon, and cross-country.

There are so many new runners today. If you are one of them, or if you are a runner who can't seem to improve, I hope you'll read this book so you can coach yourself and reach your goals in the most efficient ways possible. I think most coaches would agree with me that you cannot progress in this sport unless you know how to train— let *Road Racing for Serious Runners* be your coach. See you on the roads and at the races!

Bill Rodgers

© Stacey Cramp

PREFACE

"How can I race faster?"

What runner who has pinned on a race number hasn't asked this at some point? During our immersion in running for more than the past two decades (one of us as a world-class marathoner, coach, and exercise physiologist, the other as a writer and editor in the sport and a sub-31:00 10K runner), we've heard questions about how to run faster more than about any other topic. Everyone wants to know how to get from the starting line to the finish line in less time.

We wrote this book to answer that question. And guess what? The way to run faster isn't necessarily to run more mileage, or to run harder speed workouts. The answer is to train more intelligently—to use exercise physiology to train in the most effective way for your target distances. That's what you'll learn to do in this book, as we show you the right balance of the right types of workouts for the most popular road races, from the 5K on up to the marathon.

Read this book, and among other benefits, you will

- get week-by-week training schedules for your favorite race distance, adjusted for your level of mileage;
- learn the right pace to run during your speed workouts;
- understand why long runs are necessary and learn the right way to do them;
- see why and how to taper your training before an important race to reach your potential;
- understand how to detect and avoid staleness and injury so that you can progress in your training; and
- learn the best racing strategy and mental approach for your target distances.

Road Racing for Serious Runners is for anyone who cares enough about his or her running to want to learn how to go about it in the most effective, time-efficient way. We've written this book so that it will be as useful for a 20-mile-a-week 5K runner as for a 100-mile-a-week marathoner. Each of the race-training chapters has weekly schedules based on various levels of mileage, allowing you to benefit from them regardless of your current mileage. You'll also find that the training schedules permit you to fit your running into the rest of your life. The schedules give you a few key workouts to do each week but let you choose when within the week you do them. In other words, this book is for the legions of runners out there who struggle with how to get the most out of their limited training time.

Best wishes for good training and racing.

ACKNOWLEDGMENTS

We owe thanks to

—our wives, Christine Pfitzinger and Stacey Cramp, for their support and for tolerating frequent calls from the other's husband;

—Martin Barnard, Charlie Petit, and others at Human Kinetics for helping to bring this book to life;

—Bill Rodgers, for writing the foreword;

—the elite runners profiled in chapters 6-10, for divulging details of their training;

—Arch Jelley, Bill Dellinger, Bill Squires, Arthur Lydiard, and David Martin, PhD, all of whose philosophies influenced the training schedules in this book;

—Jack Daniels, PhD, for sharing his wisdom in successfully applying physiology to the training of distance runners;

—the American Running and Fitness Association, for offering Scott free office space; and

—whoever invented the Internet, for enabling us to complete this book while living in different hemispheres.

Pete Pfitzinger and Scott Douglas

PART I

THE PHYSIOLOGY OF RUNNING

A Multispeed Approach to Road Racing

It's fair for you to ask at the outset why you should read this book. Certainly there's no lack of running books presuming to tell you how to train, and some of them contain sound advice. Yet none except this one base all their information on indisputable exercise physiology and then show how to apply that physiology to prepare for peak performance in an easy-to-understand, adaptable format.

The philosophy behind this book is simple: To race your best, you should pick a goal race that will be the focus of a season. Then, in the weeks before that race, you should train at the right balance of intensity and distance to prepare for success at your chosen distance.

This is hardly a revolutionary approach—indeed, it's the one used by most world-class runners. Yet it's very different from how most runners go about their training and racing. Many runners seem to race haphazardly, one week running a 10-miler, the next a 5K, the following week a 10K. They tend to train in the same random way, guessing at what types of workouts to do without being able to explain how one week's track session relates to the next. As a result, they seldom approach their racing potential.

So what do smart runners know that others don't? They know that of the seemingly infinite variations of running workouts, focused training centers on just five types: (1) short, fast speedwork to improve leg turnover and running form; (2) longer repetitions of two to six minutes at 3K to 5K race pace to improve maximum oxygen uptake; (3) tempo runs of 20 to 40 minutes at 10-mile race pace to delay lactic acid buildup; (4) long runs to build endurance; and (5) easy recovery runs to allow top effort on hard days.

That's not to say that other types of training aren't helpful. If all you've ever done is run steadily and you then add some fast running once or so a week, your race performances will almost certainly improve. But smart runners know that the types of workouts we just listed deliver the best returns from precious training time.

Successful runners also know that they'll race their best if they have a goal distance around which to base their training. They know that each race distance has different physiological requirements. Once they've picked their goal distance, then, structuring their training is straightforward: They balance the five main types of workouts appropriately to prepare for the physiological demands of their goal race. With the help of this book, you can learn how to do the same with your running.

A note up-front about the term *serious runners*: Don't think that we're addressing only front-of-the-pack whippets or that what we

© Victah

have to say pertains just to the 100-miles-a-week crowd. This book is for you if you care enough about your running to want to know how to train most effectively to reach your potential in races, regardless of your speed or weekly mileage. The principles are the same for all runners who want to improve; only the numbers are different.

Multispeed Approach

Aren't we oversimplifying things by saying that there are only five important types of workouts? On what basis do we make this claim?

On the basis of research in exercise physiology. Endurance athletes, especially distance runners, have been a major focus of exercise scientists' research for more than three decades now. This work has shown that the physiological determinants of running success are few and predictable, and that most can be improved with training. Four of the five components of training listed above—short speedwork, intervals at 3K to 5K race pace, 20- to 40-minute runs at 10-mile race pace, and long runs—are the best way to develop one of those physiological determinants. The fifth type of training, recovery training, allows your body to consolidate the benefits of the four other types without breaking down. Put another way, there's sound physiology behind every workout prescribed in this book.

Training intelligently means combining these five components in the best way to stimulate the physiological adaptations necessary for your goal race. Each race is its own animal, of course, but what the distances covered in this book, from 5K and cross-country on through the marathon, have in common is that they all require some degree of the five types of training. Put another way, although you can't improve in all aspects of your physiology at the same time, neither can you ignore any type if you want to race to your potential. Again, the trick is to find the proper proportion of each component for your goal race.

Pete's Principles

Here are two weeks of my training leading up to running 2:11:54 for third place at the 1987 New York City Marathon. Eight weeks remained until the marathon at the beginning of this two-week period, so my mileage was still high.

The pattern of my training was based on the principles used in the schedules in this book—a mix of long runs, tempo runs, $\dot{V}O_2$max workouts, basic speed sessions, and recovery runs. In this case, the training primarily emphasized boosting my endurance and lactate threshold (the most important physiological determinants of success in the marathon) while not ignoring the other types of workouts.

Not that this training was perfect. I now have a much better understanding of how to balance hard workouts and recovery runs to avoid overtraining. In retrospect, my recovery days were too hard, which kept me from progressing on my hard days and led to several instances of overtraining. Today, I would reduce the mileage on recovery days and wear a heart-rate monitor on those days to ensure that I was running easily enough to allow my body to recover for the next scheduled hard workout.

	Training objective	Morning	Evening	Miles
Sunday	Long run 1	22 miles, start at 6:15/mile, build to 5:30/mile	–	22
Monday	Recovery	10 miles at 6:30/mile	6 miles at 6:15/mile	16
Tuesday	$\dot{V}O_2max$	6 miles at 6:15/mile	3-mile warm-up, 5 × 1,600 meters in 4:32 to 4:34 (jog 2:00 between), 4-mile cool-down	19
Wednesday	Long run 2	6 miles at 6:30/mile	15 miles start at 6:15/mile, build to 5:50/mile	21
Thursday	Recovery	10 miles at 6:15/mile	6 miles at 6:30/mile	16
Friday	Long run 3	5 miles at 6:15/mile	16 miles start at 6:15/mile, build to 5:40/mile	21
Saturday	Basic speed	10 miles (8 miles, followed by 10 × 100-meter strideouts, 1-mile cool-down)	6 miles at 6:15/mile	16
			Mileage for week	**131**

	Training objective	Morning	Evening	Miles
Sunday	Long run 1	20 miles start at 6:15/mile, build to 5:30/mile	–	20
Monday	Recovery	10 miles at 7:00/mile	5 miles at 6:30/mile	15
Tuesday	$\dot{V}O_2$max	8 miles at 6:00/mile	4-mile warm-up, 6 × 2:30 hard on grass (1:00 jog between), 4-mile cool-down	20
Wednesday	Long run 2	6 miles at 6:15/mile	15 miles, start at 6:15/mile, build to 5:50/mile	21
Thursday	Recovery	10 miles at 6:15/mile	8 miles at 6:15/mile	18
Friday	Recovery	9 miles at 6:15/mile	5 miles at 6:30/mile	14
Saturday	Tempo run	3-mile warm-up, 5-mile tempo run in 24:12, 4-mile cool-down	6 miles at 6:30/mile	18
			Mileage for week	**126**

How to Use This Book

With all that as preface, let's get to what you care most about—how to use this book to run faster. As we noted earlier, inherent in this book's structure is the idea that you're going to pick a distance that will be the focus of your racing season. This doesn't mean that you'll race only at this distance; indeed, the race-training schedules in chapters 6 through 10 include preparatory races at a variety of distances as you build toward your goal. It simply means that all of your preparation, including these tune-up races, is consistent with the physiological demands of your goal distance. By focusing your training in this way, we hope to help you to reach your goal.

What we're not doing is telling you what that goal should be. That is, we're not going to tell you which of the five race chapters you should focus on. Because of the combination of genetics and psychology, all runners have a narrow range of distances at which they're best. But without conducting a series of physiological tests we can't accurately say what that range is for you. Moreover, it's not as if you can't race with success at distances longer or shorter than those to which you're best suited. All runners can benefit, both physically and mentally, from focusing on a variety of races during their racing lifetimes. After all, you have more than one or two 12-week periods in your life to prepare for races. So it's up to you to pick your goal. Once you've done so, we'll help you get to it. (In the same way, it's up to you to decide how to use this book over several seasons.)

We're assuming that you've picked up this book because you want to get ready to race at a specific distance. Chapters 6 through 10 offer training schedules for five sets of common distances: 5K, 8K or 10K, 15K to half marathon, marathon, and cross-country. It's likely that you'll start by looking at the chapter for the distance that interests you most. You might have already started one of the training schedules by the time you get to reading this part of the book. That's fine—the race-training chapters are made to be self-contained. At some point, though, you should flesh out your understanding of what's in the specific race-training chapters with other information. Here's what you'll find in the rest of this book.

Background Chapters

Chapters 2 and 3 provide in-depth, usable backgrounds on the physiology of running. Chapter 2 focuses on what's commonly called speedwork. The chapter has two sections, one on $\dot{V}O_2max$, the other on basic speed. $\dot{V}O_2max$ stands for maximal oxygen uptake, or how much oxygen can be transported to and used by working muscles. It's the most important physiological attribute in determining your success in a 5K and plays a significant part in your performance all the way up to the marathon. The first section of chapter 2

Even world-class runners like Bob Kennedy rely on good base training to begin their preparations for top-flight competition.

explains what $\dot{V}O_2max$ is, what determines it, and how to improve it. The race-training schedules in chapters 6 through 10 include $\dot{V}O_2max$ training that's based on the physiological explanation in chapter 2.

The second section of chapter 2 focuses on basic speed, or how fast you can run 400 meters or shorter. Of the five components of training, basic speed is the least important for success in racing the distances covered in this book, but that doesn't mean that you should ignore it. Chapter 2 details why basic speed is important, what determines it, and how to improve it. As with $\dot{V}O_2$max, the race-training schedules in chapters 6 through 10 include basic speed training that's based on the physiological explanation in chapter 2.

The other background physiology chapter, chapter 3, focuses on endurance. It, too, has two sections—one on lactate threshold, the other on pure endurance. Your lactate threshold is how much of your $\dot{V}O_2$max you can use before you start to accumulate lactic acid. This determines how much of your $\dot{V}O_2$max you can maintain during a race. In 8Ks and 10Ks, lactate threshold is of equal importance to $\dot{V}O_2$max; it's even more important in races of 15K and longer. Although this physiological attribute might seem more related to speed than endurance, it really determines how long you can maintain a given pace; thus, it's in the endurance chapter. The first section of chapter 3 explains what lactate threshold is, what determines it, and how to improve it. The race-training schedules in chapters 6 through 10 include lactate-threshold training that's based on the physiological explanation in chapter 3.

The second section of chapter 3 focuses on pure endurance, or how long you can run without having to slow substantially. Having an adequate base of pure endurance underlies being able to compete at any of the distances in this book. Endurance is of equal importance to a high lactate threshold in marathon success. Chapter 3 explains what pure endurance is, what determines it, and how to improve it. The long runs that are part of the race-training schedules in chapters 6 through 10 are based on the physiological explanation in chapter 3.

Two other chapters precede the race-training schedules. Both contain physiologically based information that will help you get the most out of your training and racing as you progress through the schedules. Chapter 4 has sections on building your mileage, training by heart rate, physiological considerations for women runners, and avoiding overtraining, dehydration, and injury. Using this information will help you train consistently at a high level as you progress toward your goal, regardless of the distance you're focusing on.

Chapter 5 explains how to optimize your performance on race day. The schedules in chapters 6 through 10 will get you to the starting line of your goal race with the appropriate blend of speed and endurance, but they won't stop you from jeopardizing your performance with simple mistakes during the race or in the few days before it. So before your goal race, you'll want to read chapter 5, which covers racing tactics, warming up and cooling down, glycogen (carbohydrate) loading, tapering, and recovery.

Race-Training Chapters

Chapters 6 through 10—training to race 5K, 8K or 10K, 15K to half marathon, marathon, and cross-country—are the heart of this book. Here's what's in each chapter.

Each of the race-training chapters provides a look at the physiology of the event. This makes sense given that the training schedules are based on the physiological demands of the distance. You'll learn the relative importance of the four physiological attributes discussed in chapters 2 and 3 in your chosen distance, as well as how the emphasis among them changes as your goal race approaches. Once you know the physiology of your chosen distance, then you can better understand why the schedules have you doing specific workouts.

Next, the race-training chapters provide conversions from other distances to the distance that's the subject of the chapter. This will help you set challenging but realistic goals. The tables in the appendix provide further information about conversions. The exception is chapter 10, the cross-country chapter, because time is relatively meaningless in cross-country races.

The schedules follow. Chapters 6 through 9 each offer three schedules; chapter 10 is again the exception. Because chapters 6 through 9 are based on training for specific distances, their schedules are based on a range of weekly training mileage. For example, chapter 6, the 5K chapter, has schedules for runners who train less than 20 miles per week, for those who train 20 to 40 miles per week, and for those who train more than 40 miles per week. Chapters 7 through 9 use the same format, but the weekly mileage ranges increase as the race distances get longer. For example, the three ranges in the marathon chapter are less than 40 miles per week, 40 to 60 miles per week, and more than 60 miles per week. In these chapters, the three schedules are termed A (the one with the lowest weekly mileage), B (the one with the middle range of weekly mileage), and C (the one with the highest weekly mileage). We leave it to your training background, ambition, injury history, and available time to decide which of the weekly mileage schedules to follow.

© Victah

Cross-country racing requires training specific to the demands of off-road running.

The schedules in chapter 10, the cross-country chapter, are a bit different because the chapter prepares you for a type of racing, not a set race distance. Just as there's more than one distance for road races, so too for cross-country. So chapter 10 provides four schedules to reflect that range. Two are to prepare for cross-country races that are 3K to 7K long. These are termed schedules A-1 (less than 35 miles per week) and A-2 (more than 35 miles per week). The other schedules are to prepare for cross-country races that are 8K to 12K long. These are termed schedules B-1 (less than 45 miles per week) and B-2 (more than 45 miles per week).

The schedules are constructed in a weekly format that builds your training toward your goal race. They're easy to read both horizontally and vertically. Horizontally, the schedules detail the key workouts in each week, as determined by which physiological attributes are important to develop at that time in your training. Read across, the schedules tell you how many weeks there are until your goal race, your longest run for the week, your second longest run for the week, your lactate threshold or $\dot{V}O_2$max workout for the week, your basic speed workout for the week, and what your total mileage should be for the week.

Read vertically, the schedules show how each of the types of key workouts progresses as you approach your goal race. In the schedules with the highest weekly mileage (schedule C in chapters 6 through 9, schedules A-2 and B-2 in chapter 10), the last column reads "Percentage of peak." This is the percentage of the highest week's mileage in the schedule. This column is for runners following those schedules who want to do more than the mileage prescribed in the schedule. It ensures that they follow the principle that underlies all the schedules—gradually building mileage and then reducing it as the goal race approaches.

In each of the race-training chapters, the five key workouts—longest run, second longest run, lactate-threshold workouts, $\dot{V}O_2$max workouts, and basic speed—are briefly explained. These sections, abbreviated versions of the relevant information from chapters 2 and 3, explain how the types of workouts are structured for a given chapter's race distance. After these brief refreshers on the main workouts, we'll show you how to put them together to make a week's training that balances hard work with recovery.

Each of the race chapters also contains advice on racing tactics and mental approach. Although the racing-tactics section in chapter 5 applies to all the distances covered in the book, each race-training chapter adds useful information specific to the distance being discussed.

Finally, the race-training chapters contain brief profiles of world-class runners known for their prowess in the race that's the subject of the chapter. These profiles will help you see how leading runners incorporate the principles in that chapter's schedules in their preparation to race against the best runners in the world.

CHAPTER 2

Training to Improve V̇O₂max and Speed

© Victah

Most racers know that for top performance they need to do more than log the miles. So they head to the track or roads and punish themselves with grueling bouts of "speedwork," without being able to state why they're doing the workouts other than that they are working "to get faster." Certainly, some fast running will help them race better than none.

But for all their hard work, they usually aren't maximizing their training time. In this chapter, we'll show you why and how to improve the two main components of racing fitness that runners try to develop with hard workouts—$\dot{V}O_2$max and basic speed.

Improving $\dot{V}O_2$max

Many serious runners know that improving $\dot{V}O_2$max, or aerobic capacity, is key to racing better. But what's the best way to boost it? High mileage? Hill workouts? Hard quarters twice a week? Mile repeats? Let's start to understand how to improve your $\dot{V}O_2$max by looking closely at what it is.

Defining $\dot{V}O_2$max

Think of $\dot{V}O_2$max as the capacity of your body's plumbing for aerobic exercise. Runners with a high $\dot{V}O_2$max have a plumbing system that allows them to pump large amounts of oxygen-rich blood to working muscles. With training, you can maximize the size of your pump and the quantity of blood that it transports.

More precisely, your $\dot{V}O_2$max is the maximal amount of oxygen that your heart can pump to your muscles and that your muscles can then use to produce energy. It's the product of your heart rate times the amount of blood pumped per beat times the proportion of oxygen extracted from the blood and used by your muscles. The combination of your training and your genetics determines how high a $\dot{V}O_2$max you have.

Your $\dot{V}O_2$max is important because it determines your aerobic capacity—the higher your $\dot{V}O_2$max, the greater your ability to produce energy aerobically. Everything else being equal, the more energy you can produce aerobically, the faster a pace you can maintain. $\dot{V}O_2$max is the most important physiological variable determining performance in races of 1,500 meters to 5,000 meters. $\dot{V}O_2$max is also an important physiological variable for longer races, but the longer the race, the more important lactate threshold becomes relative to $\dot{V}O_2$max in determining performance.

With the right training, you can improve most of the determinants of your $\dot{V}O_2$max.

The first determinant of $\dot{V}O_2$max is maximal heart rate. Your maximal heart rate is determined by genetics and tends to decrease with age. Recent evidence, however, suggests that maximal heart rate doesn't decrease as rapidly with age in people who maintain cardiovascular fitness. You can't, however, increase your maximal heart rate with training.

The second determinant of $\dot{V}O_2$max is the amount of blood that the left ventricle of your heart can pump with each contraction. Known as stroke volume, this factor, unlike maximal heart rate, increases with the right type of training. Increased stroke volume is the primary adaptation that improves your $\dot{V}O_2$max with training. Together, your maximal heart rate (number of beats per minute) times your stroke volume (quantity of blood pumped with each heart beat) determines your cardiac output, which is the quantity of oxygen-rich blood pumped by your heart per minute.

The final determinant of $\dot{V}O_2$max is the proportion of oxygen in the blood that's used. This is the amount of oxygen in your arterial blood minus the amount of oxygen in your venous blood, which represents the amount of oxygen extracted by the tissues. One adaptation to training is that your tissues can extract more oxygen from arterial blood, leaving your venous blood with a lower percentage of oxygen than that in untrained people. This happens because training increases both the blood flow to the working muscles and the number of capillaries providing oxygen-rich blood to individual muscle cells.

For sports like running, in which you propel your body over the ground, $\dot{V}O_2$max is expressed relative to body weight. The units used are milliliters of oxygen consumed per kilogram of body weight per minute (ml/kg/min). Typical $\dot{V}O_2$max values for sedentary 35-year-old men and women are 45 ml/kg/min and 38 ml/kg/min, respectively. World-class male 5,000 meter runners tend to have $\dot{V}O_2$max values of 75–85 ml/kg/min. World-class male marathoners tend to have somewhat lower $\dot{V}O_2$max values, generally in the range of 70–75 ml/kg/min; they achieve their performances through higher lactate thresholds, which we'll discuss in chapter 3.

Women tend to have lower $\dot{V}O_2$max values than men because women generally have higher essential body-fat stores and lower hemoglobin levels than men. Because $\dot{V}O_2$max is expressed relative to body weight, the larger essential fat stores in women are a disadvantage. Hemoglobin is a protein in red blood cells that carries oxygen to the tissues. With less hemoglobin, women have less oxygen per unit of blood. The $\dot{V}O_2$max values of well-trained women are typically about 10 percent lower than those of well-trained men.

Table 2.1 How $\dot{V}O_2$max Increases With Training

	Maximal heart rate	Stroke volume	Oxygen extraction
Improves with training?	No	Yes	Yes

Table 2.2   Typical $\dot{V}O_2$max Values

	$\dot{V}O_2$max (ml/kg/min)
Sedentary 35-year-old man	45
Sedentary 35-year-old woman	38
World-class male 5K runner	79
World-class female 5K runner	70
World-class male marathoner	73
World-class female marathoner	65

With six months to a year of training, our sedentary examples could expect to increase their $\dot{V}O_2$max values by 20 to 30 percent. In all cases, training improves $\dot{V}O_2$max within a genetically determined range. That is, your $\dot{V}O_2$max will increase with training, but eventually the rate of improvement will decrease as you approach your genetic potential. If you've been training for several years, increases in $\dot{V}O_2$max are hard won. That's why it's even more important for veteran runners than relative beginners to train as detailed below to maximize their $\dot{V}O_2$max.

Improving $\dot{V}O_2$max

The greatest stimulus to improving $\dot{V}O_2$max comes by training at an intensity that requires 95 to 100 percent of your current $\dot{V}O_2$max. How do you know what that is? You can find out by having your $\dot{V}O_2$max measured at an exercise physiology lab. In this test, you start running slowly on a treadmill. The speed or incline of the treadmill is then increased every few minutes until you can't keep up, and the air you exhale is collected and analyzed. The test usually takes about 10 to 15 minutes.

If you don't have access to a lab, you can make an educated guess of your $\dot{V}O_2$max running pace based on your racing times. Your running speed at 95 to 100 percent of your $\dot{V}O_2$max should be about your 3,000- to 5,000-meter race pace. Doing a portion of your training at this pace, therefore, will provide the greatest stimulus to improving your $\dot{V}O_2$max—you'll stress your cardiovascular system to its limit, which will help to increase your stroke volume and improve your ability to extract oxygen from the blood.

The biggest boosts to $\dot{V}O_2$max come from training within a narrow range of intensity.

You can also estimate the appropriate intensity for $\dot{V}O_2$max training based on your heart rate. $\dot{V}O_2$max training pace coincides with approximately 95 to 98 percent of your heart-rate reserve or maximal heart rate. (For an explanation of heart-rate-based training, definition of heart-rate reserve, and so on, see "Using Heart Rate to Monitor Your Training" in chapter 4.) You should keep your heart rate several beats under your maximum during this type of training. Otherwise, you'll work too intensely, which will shorten the workout and tend to provide less stimulus to improving $\dot{V}O_2$max.

Your body can respond positively to only a limited amount of training at $\dot{V}O_2$max intensity before it tends to break down. It reaches a point where it can't recover from and adapt to your hard work. Ideally, you'll find a balance of the volume of training per $\dot{V}O_2$max workout and the frequency of these workouts. The goal is to train at $\dot{V}O_2$max intensity often enough to improve but not so often that you become overtrained. The schedules in chapters 6 through 10 use the following guidelines to create the optimal stimulus to improving $\dot{V}O_2$max.

Volume of training per workout   You'll improve $\dot{V}O_2$max most rapidly by running $2\frac{1}{2}$ to 5 miles (4,000 to 8,000 meters) of intervals per workout. The optimal volume within that range depends on your training history. If you run less than $2\frac{1}{2}$ miles of intervals, you'll still provide a training stimulus, but your rate of improvement will be slower. If you try to run much more than 5 miles of intervals at this intensity (good luck), it's likely that either you will be unable to maintain the appropriate pace for the entire workout or you will become so worn out from the workout that you won't recover quickly enough for your next one. For most runners, workouts of 3 to $4\frac{1}{2}$ miles (4,800 to 7,200 meters) of intervals provide the most effective balance.

Frequency of workouts   You'll improve $\dot{V}O_2$max most rapidly by running one high-volume workout at 95 to 100 percent of $\dot{V}O_2$max per week. Depending on the distance you'll be racing and the number of weeks out from your goal race, it may be beneficial to complete a second lower-volume $\dot{V}O_2$max workout during certain weeks.

Duration of intervals   You'll improve $\dot{V}O_2$max most rapidly by running repetitions of two to six minutes duration. For most runners, this means intervals of approximately 600 to 1,600 meters, or one mile. Besides going to a track, you can also do your $\dot{V}O_2$max workouts running uphills, on a golf course, and so forth. When training for cross-country, for instance, it's best to try to simulate race conditions closely during your $\dot{V}O_2$max workouts.

You achieve the greatest stimulus to improving aerobic capacity by getting your cardiovascular system up to 95 to 100 percent of $\dot{V}O_2$max and maintaining it in that range for as long as you can during the workout. Short intervals aren't nearly as effective in providing this stimulus because you don't accumulate enough time in the optimal intensity range. For example, if you run 400-meter repeats, it'll be easy to hold $\dot{V}O_2$max pace, but you'll only be at that pace for a short time during each interval. As a result, you'll have to run many

400s to provide much stimulus to improve your $\dot{V}O_2$max. If, on the other hand, you run 1,200-meter repeats at the correct pace, your cardiovascular system will be at 95 to 100 percent of $\dot{V}O_2$max for several minutes during each interval. During the workout you'll accumulate more time at the most effective training intensity.

Speed of intervals $\dot{V}O_2$max workouts are most effective—that is, they provide the greatest stimulus to improving $\dot{V}O_2$max—when you do them at a speed that falls between your 3,000-meter race pace and your 5,000-meter pace. It's within this window that you're most likely to be working at 95 to 100 percent of your $\dot{V}O_2$max. If you run slower than that, then you're heading toward lactate-threshold training territory. As we'll see in chapter 3, lactate-threshold training is valuable, but your $\dot{V}O_2$max workouts aren't the times to do it!

Similarly, if you run your intervals faster than the 95 to 100 percent of $\dot{V}O_2$max training range, you won't provide as great a stimulus to improve your $\dot{V}O_2$max for two reasons. First, when you run faster than $\dot{V}O_2$max pace, you increasingly use your anaerobic system, which stimulates that system to improve. You might think that the anaerobic system is just as important as the aerobic system, and it is—if you're racing 800 meters. But if you're racing 5,000 meters or farther, you use the anaerobic system primarily for the kick at the end of the race. If you've trained aerobically while equally talented runners have trained anaerobically, you'll be so far ahead going into the kick that you won't have to worry about their finishing speed.

The other reason that running your intervals too fast provides less stimulus to improve $\dot{V}O_2$max is that you simply can't do as much volume. Remember, the total amount of time accumulated at $\dot{V}O_2$max is what's important. Let's say you run four repetitions of 800 meters at your 1,500-meter race pace, running each repeat in 2:24. You'll be tired after that workout, but you'll have done less than 10 minutes of work, of which perhaps 6 minutes were at the most effective intensity to improving $\dot{V}O_2$max. If, however, you read this book and decide to run five repetitions of 1,200 meters at your 5,000-meter race pace, running your repeats in 4:00, you'll have completed 20 minutes of hard running (see table 2.3). Almost all of your work will be at the appropriate intensity to stimulate improvements in your $\dot{V}O_2$max.

Duration of recovery between intervals   The duration of recovery between intervals should be long enough to allow your heart rate to go down to 55 percent of heart-rate reserve or 65 percent of maximal heart rate. If you cut the rest too short, you'll likely need to shorten the workout and won't obtain as great a training stimulus. A too-

Table 2.3 Why Faster Isn't Necessarily Better for Boosting $\dot{V}O_2$max		
	Workout 1	**Workout 2**
Speed of interval	2:30 (1,500-meter race pace)	4:00 (5K race pace)
Length of interval	800 meters	1,200 meters
Number of intervals	4	5
Amount of hard running	<10 minutes	20 minutes
Amount of time at right intensity to improve $\dot{V}O_2$max	About 6 minutes	Almost 20 minutes
Good workout to improve $\dot{V}O_2$max	**No**	**Yes**

short rest might also mean that you'll have to run subsequent intervals too anaerobically, which, as we saw above, isn't the point of $\dot{V}O_2$max workouts. If your rest is too long, however, the training stimulus will also be reduced.

The optimal amount of recovery between intervals depends on the length of the intervals you're running. As a general guideline, the rest between intervals should be from 50 to 90 percent of the time it takes to run the interval. For example, if Colleen is running 1,200-meter repeats in 4:30, her recovery jog should last 50 to 90 percent of this time, or between 2:15 and 4:00.

Between intervals, resist the temptation to stand bent over with your hands on your knees. Although it sounds counterintuitive, research has shown that you recover most quickly when you jog during your recovery because doing so helps clear lactic acid from your blood.

Designing the workout   The ideal workout to stimulate $\dot{V}O_2$max consists of $2\frac{1}{2}$ to 5 miles (4,000 to 8,000 meters) of intervals of two to six minutes duration at approximately 95 to 100 percent of $\dot{V}O_2$max. Within these parameters, you can structure workouts through various combinations of intervals. $\dot{V}O_2$max workouts fall into two basic categories—workouts in which the distance of the interval is constant and workouts in which it's varied.

Many coaches vary the length of intervals within a workout to make the workout easier mentally. Many self-coached runners do the same, running "ladder" workouts that consist of one interval each at a variety of distances on the way up and down the ladder. They then talk themselves through the workout piece by piece, telling themselves, "OK, just one mile repeat, then each one gets shorter on the way down." This approach can backfire because an important element of training is preparing mentally for the race. Running a set of intervals of the same length is preferable because you learn what it feels like to maintain speed while fatigue increases, which more

Elana Meyer prepares for world-class competition with regular $\dot{V}O_2$max sessions.

closely simulates a race. There are times, however, when varying the length of the intervals can be beneficial, such as running some shorter, quicker intervals at the end of the workout to improve your kick.

Another instance in which you might vary the length of your intervals is if you're doing a fartlek session, a loosely structured workout of alternating hard surges with recovery jogs. Cross-country runners, who benefit from doing their $\dot{V}O_2$max workouts on the surfaces on which they race, are most likely to do fartleks on a regular basis. For more on fartlek, see the cross-country training schedules in chapter 10.

Examples of workouts that will most effectively improve $\dot{V}O_2$max are presented in table 2.4.

You would run each of these workouts at 3,000- to 5,000-meter race pace with a recovery jog until your heart rate slows to 55 percent of heart-rate reserve or 65 percent of maximal heart rate. Remember that the best pace for these workouts is within a range between 3K and 5K race pace. Do the shorter intervals toward the 3K race pace end of the range, the longer ones toward the 5K race pace end. (In other words, don't run five 1-mile repeats at 3K race pace.)

Harder Isn't Always Better

Many ambitious runners will tell you that the workouts just described are good but that you could train harder by running the intervals faster, reducing the rest interval, or both. And they're right—the workout would be harder. It would also be less effective.

Table 2.4 Examples of $\dot{V}O_2$max Workouts

Length of interval	Number of intervals	Total distance
600 meters	7 to 10	4,200 to 6,000 meters
800 meters	6 to 10	4,800 to 8,000 meters
1,000 meters	5 to 8	5,000 to 8,000 meters
1,200 meters	4 to 6	4,800 to 7,200 meters
1,600 meters (1 mile)	3 to 5	4,800 to 8,000 meters

Remember, the main theme of this book is that each race distance stresses various physiological attributes and that you will maximize your potential at a given distance by developing the appropriate physiological attributes. The most effective training isn't necessarily the most physically demanding training.

Let's consider Mark, who runs 15:45, or roughly 5:05 per mile, for 5K. Under the program presented here, a good VO_2max workout for Mark would be eight 800-meter repeats in 2:28 to 2:32, with a recovery jog of 1:15 to 2:00. Yet Mark can, and therefore does, run his 800-meter repeats in 2:22 or faster, with only a 1:00 rest. Asks Mark, "How could this not be a better workout?"

The answer is, "A better workout for what?" If Mark wants to train his anaerobic system, then his faster workout, with shorter recovery, is the way to go because he'll be running much of his workout anaerobically. But if Mark's goal is to improve his aerobic system— the one he will stress most in his target races of 5K to 10K—then his hard work on the track is partly in vain. He's not boosting his VO_2max as much as he could and is therefore limiting his potential in races.

Mark's experience, and that of his training partners, bears this out. They wonder why they consistently race slower than their workout times would predict, while a friend who lags in workouts but is training at his VO_2max pace beats them when it counts in races. Also, Mark's excessively hard work on the track in the middle of the week likely leaves him too tired to recover in time for his weekend races. His friend who does workouts at the hard-but-proper pace can absorb the benefits of his training and recover enough in a few days to race well on the weekend.

Improving Your Basic Speed

Obviously, the shorter the race, the more important your flat-out speed. When you're racing 100 meters, it's pretty much all that matters. At the other extreme, many marathoners figure that their basic speed has no relevance for a race that lasts more than two hours. But in races of 5K and even longer, honing your basic speed is an important aspect of preparing for peak performance.

Defining Basic Speed

Your basic speed is how fast you can run 400 meters or less. In other words, your basic speed determines how fast a pace you

© Stacey Cramp

Basic speed is determined partly by your ratio of fast-twitch to slow-twitch muscle fibers, which varies widely even among runners with similar race times.

can attain but not how fast a pace you can maintain. Speed is determined by stride frequency times stride length. Increase your stride frequency or your stride length (while holding the other constant), and you run faster. When you're running as fast as you can, both factors limit your maximal speed.

Your maximal stride frequency is determined mostly by the ratio of fast-twitch to slow-twitch fibers in your muscles. The best marathoners tend to have mostly slow-twitch muscle fibers, which, as we'll see in chapter 3, is an advantage for endurance. The best sprinters have primarily fast-twitch fibers, which allows them to have a greater stride frequency. You can't increase the number of your fast-twitch muscle fibers with training, but you can increase the size of those fibers and their ability to help you run fast.

Your stride length when you're running at top speed is determined by the length of your legs, your flexibility, and the power your legs can generate. You can't do much about the length of your legs, but you can work on both flexibility and power.

Understanding Basic Speed

Among the four types of training that improve racing performance, basic speed is the least important for distance runners. It's really paramount only in the last 200 meters of a race, when it's time to kick to the finish line. This means that you shouldn't make speed training a large component of your training schedule, but if you compete, you ignore speed at your peril. Speed training is more important for cross-country or a 5K than for a marathon, but it has a place in your training program regardless of what distance you're focusing on.

Speed training provides three benefits to a distance runner. First, it activates your fast-twitch muscle fibers and increases their glycolytic enzyme activity. This means that you improve your ability to produce energy anaerobically, boosting your sprint speed and thereby helping you to outkick your competitors. Second, by doing speed workouts and concentrating on maintaining good running form, you'll tend to improve your running form and posture at all speeds, and may improve your running economy. Third, if you do intense speed workouts, you'll increase the ability of your muscles to buffer lactic acid, so you'll be able to run anaerobically longer before having to slow. You'll therefore by able to start your finishing kick earlier.

Because this book focuses on races of 5,000 meters and longer, the workouts to improve basic speed are simple. Runners competing in shorter events will need to put a greater emphasis on speed workouts.

Improving Leg Speed

Within the limits imposed by your muscle fibers, you can improve your speed by increasing strength and flexibility and by doing workouts that help you realize the full potential of your leg turnover.

Speed is controlled by the neuromuscular system. In large part, your muscles determine how fast you can run, but the nervous system input to your muscles also plays a role. Simply stated, by running fast you teach your nervous system to let you run fast. This is why some coaches have their athletes run speed sessions down a gentle hill. The slight extra effect of gravity pushing you downhill helps your legs turn over more quickly. Running on the flat will then seem easier because your muscles have learned to turn over that much faster.

You can also improve your basic speed by improving your leg strength. You can accomplish this in several ways, including lifting weights, doing bounding or plyometric exercises, and running up hills. Running up hills is the best choice for most distance runners because it has the lowest risk of injury. Hill work also provides excellent cardiovascular training. And for cross-country runners and road racers, hill running simulates a part of competition that often determines who wins the race.

One of the most enjoyable and beneficial speed workouts for a distance runner is a set of strideouts. After a good warm-up, run several laps of a track in which you accelerate the straightaways and jog the turns. If you run eight laps, you'll do 16 accelerations of approximately 100 meters each. The key is to accelerate smoothly up to full speed, then hold your maximal speed for 40 to 50 meters. It's not necessary to monitor your heart rate for this type of workout because your accelerations are short enough that your heart rate is still increasing when you slow to a jog.

Don't run so fast that you start to tighten up. When doing striders, you don't want to practice straining because that won't transfer to running relaxed at other speeds. By using the first part of each strider to build to full speed, you should be able to avoid tying up.

Concentrate on maintaining good running form and staying relaxed when doing this workout. It's important to avoid tensing up your neck, shoulders, and arms. Because it's nearly impossible to think about all facets of good running form at once, focus on one element during each strider. For example, concentrate in turn on keeping your jaw loose, driving with your arms forward and backward, pushing off the balls of your feet, maintaining good posture, keeping your shoulders relaxed, and so on.

As mentioned earlier, you can also work on your speed by doing this workout on a slight downhill. Be careful, however, because it's easy to strain a muscle when running fast downhill, particularly if you haven't done much speedwork recently. Try this workout on a gentle downhill on a soft surface such as grass. If you don't have access to soft surfaces and going to a track isn't convenient, you can do striders on a flat stretch of road.

Hill training can improve many aspects of your performance.

You'll get the greatest benefits of increased speed and improved form by doing your speed training on one of your moderate training days. That is, don't do this workout the day after a hard track session or a long run, when you want to maximize recovery. (And certainly don't do it on your hard days.) Rather, plan your striders when you're a couple days past a hard workout and at least one day before your next hard one. It's OK to do speed training the day before a long run; many runners find that they feel better on their long runs when they've done striders the day before.

Of course, all the $\dot{V}O_2$max and basic speed sessions in the world won't help you to race your best if you can't cover the distance. Success in the races covered in this book requires not only a solid base of endurance (what we're calling pure endurance) but also the ability to cover that distance at a speed that's a high percentage of your $\dot{V}O_2$max (your lactate threshold). Improving your pure endurance and lactate threshold are the subjects of the next chapter.

CHAPTER 3

Training to Improve Lactate Threshold and Pure Endurance

© Victah

In any race, you must overcome two elements—the distance itself, which requires pure endurance, and the tendency to slow, which requires a high lactate threshold. This chapter explains how to improve your racing performances with training that optimally develops these two key components of successful distance running.

Lactate-Threshold Training

Many serious runners talk about doing lactate-threshold training, tempo runs, and so forth. But they usually talk in vague terms. They may call an eight-miler that they run harder than usual a tempo run, even though the latter term has to do with a specific physiological concept. Let's look at what lactate threshold is to see how to improve it and, therefore, race better.

Defining Lactate Threshold

Your lactate threshold (LT) determines how fast you can race. When you select a race pace, you really select a pace that prevents the accumulation of lactate (a by-product of carbohydrate metabolism). When you are resting, walking, or running slowly, the amount of lactate in your blood remains low and relatively constant because the rate of lactate entering your blood is equal to the rate at which it's removed. As you progress from rest to walking to easy running, both the rate of lactate production by your muscles and the rate of clearance by various body tissues increase. When you exercise above a certain intensity, however, the rate of lactate formation is greater than the rate of clearance, so the lactate concentration rises in your muscles and blood. This is your lactate threshold, the exercise intensity above which lactate clearance can no longer keep up with lactate production.

Your lactate threshold is the most important factor in determining running performance in races longer than 10K. For the 10K, $\dot{V}O_2$max and lactate threshold are about equally important. For the 5K, a high $\dot{V}O_2$max is the most important physiological attribute, but a high lactate threshold is still important.

Understanding Lactate Threshold

Exercise physiologists used to think that $\dot{V}O_2$max was the most valid physiological variable for predicting distance-running performance. When Jack Daniels and his colleagues investigated changes in $\dot{V}O_2$max and running performance with training, however, they found that running performance continued to improve after $\dot{V}O_2$max ceased to improve (Daniels 1978). That's because you can continue to boost your lactate threshold long after you've maximized gains in $\dot{V}O_2$max. That's good news for veteran runners.

Oxygen consumption at the lactate threshold is known as your $LT\dot{V}O_2$. During the past 20 years, research has shown that $LT\dot{V}O_2$ is more accurate than $\dot{V}O_2$max in predicting distance-running performance. Pace at the lactate threshold (LT pace), which also accounts for differences between individuals in running economy, is even more accurate in predicting distance-running performance. For example, a study with distance runners by Peter Farrell and colleagues

Long-time runners like Amy Rudolph can continue to improve their performances by boosting their lactate threshold.

found that measuring the LT pace predicted 94 percent of the variation in racing speed, compared to only 79 percent by variation in $\dot{V}O_2$max (Farrell et al. 1979). Higher correlation occurs between LT measurements and endurance performance than between $\dot{V}O_2$max and endurance performance because $\dot{V}O_2$max primarily reflects the ability of the heart to transport oxygen to the muscles, whereas the lactate threshold also reflects adaptations in the muscles that increase the capacity of those muscles to produce energy aerobically.

Studies have shown that LT pace is directly determined by just two factors: your oxygen consumption at the lactate threshold ($LT\dot{V}O_2$) and your running economy. A study using competitive cyclists found $LT\dot{V}O_2$ and economy to explain 99 percent of the variance in LT pace.

To illustrate the advantage of a high $LT\dot{V}O_2$, let's compare two runners who have identical $\dot{V}O_2$max values of 60 ml/kg/min but different lactate thresholds (see table 3.1). (Oxygen consumption is measured as milliliters of oxygen consumed per kilogram of body weight per minute.) Kristina's $LT\dot{V}O_2$ occurs at 48 ml/kg/min (80 percent of $\dot{V}O_2$max), while Amy's $LT\dot{V}O_2$ occurs at 42 ml/kg/min (70 percent of $\dot{V}O_2$max). If the two runners try to race at a speed that requires 45 ml/kg/min, Kristina will be able to maintain that pace, but Amy will build up lactic acid and will have to slow.

Running Economy

$LT\dot{V}O_2$ isn't the answer by itself, however, because we don't all use the same amount of oxygen at a given speed. Just as some cars consume gasoline more economically than others, some runners are more economical than others in consuming oxygen. That is, a more economical runner consumes less oxygen to maintain a specific pace.

Table 3.1   Two Runners With the Same $\dot{V}O_2$max but Different Lactate Thresholds

	$\dot{V}O_2$max	Lactate threshold	Able to race at pace that requires 45 ml/kg/min?
Kristina	60 ml/kg/min	48 (80% of max)	Yes
Amy	60 ml/kg/min	42 (70% of max)	No

Your running economy determines how fast you can run using a given amount of oxygen. If you can run faster than another runner while using the same amount of oxygen, then you're more economical. Running economy can also be viewed as how much oxygen you require to run at a given speed. If you use less oxygen while running at the same speed as another runner, then you're more economical.

For example, say two runners with identical $LT\dot{V}O_2$ values of 50 ml/kg/min are racing at a pace of 5:20 per mile. Sounds like they should both be working equally hard, right? Not necessarily. Suppose that Greg has an oxygen requirement of 47 ml/kg/min at that pace and Carter requires 53 ml/kg/min (see table 3.2). Greg will be comfortably below $LT\dot{V}O_2$ and should be able to maintain the pace, but Carter will start to accumulate lactic acid and will have to slow. In this case, Greg has a faster LT pace because he uses his $LT\dot{V}O_2$ more economically.

The primary determinants of running economy appear to be the proportion of slow-twitch versus fast-twitch fibers in your muscles and the combined effect of your biomechanics. In a study with competitive cyclists, Edward Coyle found that differences in the proportion of slow-twitch muscle fibers between athletes explained 58 percent of the variation in economy (Coyle et al. 1992). Slow-twitch fibers use oxygen more efficiently, and the better cyclists had more slow-twitch fibers. Similarly, the best marathoners and 10K runners tend to be more economical and to have more slow-twitch fibers than their slower competitors.

Running economy is also related to several biomechanical variables, such as the length of your femur relative to your tibia, but no single aspect of biomechanics has been shown to have a large impact on economy. It seems likely that interactions occur among biomechanical variables, so that the total of how you're put together is more important than any one aspect in isolation.

Table 3.2   Comparison of Two Runners' Economy

	$LT\dot{V}O_2$	Oxygen needed at 5:20-per-mile pace	Able to maintain pace?
Greg	50 ml/kg/min	47 ml/kg/min	**Yes**
Carter	50 ml/kg/min	53 ml/kg/min	**No**

Veteran runners like Rod Dixon often have an excellent running economy.

How do you improve running economy? Although there's evidence that it improves with training, the secrets of improving running economy have been elusive. The most important factor for improving economy may be the number of years that you've been running rather than the specific types of workouts that you run. Don Morgan, who has conducted a large number of studies on running economy, explains, "At this point, we do not know enough to be able to prescribe training programs to improve running economy. We may find out that different types of training improve economy depending on the strengths and weaknesses of the individual runner."

Determining Lactate Threshold

The best way to find your lactate threshold is to be tested in an exercise physiology lab. During an LT test in a lab, you run for several minutes at several different speeds. The lactate concentration in your blood is measured by pricking your finger and analyzing a couple drops of blood. A typical lactate-threshold test consists of six increasingly fast stages of five minutes each, with one minute between stages to obtain a blood sample. The first stage is slower than marathon pace, and the last stage is at about 5K race pace. By graphing your blood lactate concentration at various running speeds, the physiologist can tell you the pace and heart rate that coincide with your lactate threshold.

If you don't have access to a lab, you can conduct an LT test on a treadmill or track with the Accusport portable lactate analyzer (made by Boehringer Mannheim) or the LacTest instant lactate test (made by JWT). The Accusport is a do-it-yourself version that has been shown to have comparable accuracy to lab tests. At a cost of several hundred dollars, it's less expensive than the lactate analyzers used in labs, but still pricey, unless you and a group of running buddies buy one in tandem. The LacTest is a less expensive, disposable device.

The lower-tech method to estimate your lactate threshold is to use your race times. If you're an experienced runner, your LT pace will be approximately your race pace for 15K to the half marathon. This is because the lactate threshold determines the pace that you can maintain for races of these distances. (For shorter races, you can exceed your lactate threshold somewhat, while for the marathon you're most likely running slightly under your lactate threshold.) If

Table 3.3   Typical Lactate-Threshold Values

	Lactate threshold (percentage of $\dot{V}O_2max$)
Sedentary person	60
Recreational runner	73
World-class 5K runner	82
World-class marathoner	89

your experience is mostly with shorter races, LT pace is roughly 10 to 15 seconds per mile slower than 10K race pace.

You can also estimate the appropriate pace to stimulate improvements in your lactate threshold based on heart rate. Lactate-threshold pace generally occurs at approximately 80 to 90 percent of heart-rate reserve, which is about 85 to 92 percent of maximal heart rate. Because the relationship between lactate threshold and heart rate varies depending on genetics and fitness, however, your 15K to half-marathon race pace is probably a more accurate estimate. You can then find the heart rate that coincides with that pace.

Improving Lactate Threshold

Although lactate-threshold training is the most important type of training for distance runners, many runners don't understand how to improve their lactate threshold. The best way to do so is simple—train at, or just slightly above, your lactate threshold. Although lactate-threshold training may seem like a form of speedwork, it's more accurate to view it as a determinant of your endurance, the ability to maintain a pace for a prolonged distance. That's why it's appropriate to include it in this chapter on improving endurance, even though training to improve lactate threshold involves running significantly faster than on distance workouts.

LT workouts are of three basic types, all of which you run at the pace that coincides with your lactate threshold. The objective of these workouts is to run hard enough that lactate is just starting to accumulate in your blood. If you train at a lower intensity, there won't be as great a stimulus to improve lactate-threshold pace. If you train faster than lactate-threshold pace, you'll accumulate lactate rapidly, which won't train your muscles to work hard without accumulating lactate. As we saw with $\dot{V}O_2max$ training in chapter 2, training most effectively doesn't necessarily mean training as hard as possible. Rather, as with training to improve $\dot{V}O_2max$, the more time that you spend at the proper intensity, the greater the training stimulus.

The training schedules in chapters 6 through 10 include the appropriate volume and frequency of LT workouts to improve performance at those racing distances. These schedules will provide a training stimulus to improve your lactate threshold while preventing overtraining. The three main types of LT workouts are tempo runs, LT intervals, and LT hills. In all cases, LT workouts should feel "comfortably hard." This means that you should feel as if you're

Using a heart rate monitor allows you to do lactate threshold workouts away from the track.

working at a pretty high level, but at a level you can sustain; if you were to increase your pace by 10 seconds or more per mile, you would have to slow within the next few minutes. If you're sore and stiff the day after an LT workout, you've run too hard.

Tempo runs   The classic workout to improve your lactate threshold is the tempo run, a continuous run of 20 to 40 minutes at LT pace. An example of a tempo-run workout is an easy two-mile warm-up, four miles at 15K to half-marathon race pace, and a short cool-down jog. You can do this workout on the track or roads. At first, it's a good idea to do tempo runs on the track or other accurately measured courses, so that you have a way of checking your pace. If you wear a heart monitor on an accurately measured course, you can use the heart rate you reached to determine the proper intensity for subsequent tempo runs. Whatever the method, after a few tempo runs you should have a feel for your LT pace. Studies have shown that most runners can reliably produce this pace once they have learned it. Low-key races of 5K to 10K make a great substitute for tempo runs. Just be careful not to get carried away and race all out.

LT intervals   Rather than doing a continuous tempo run, you can gain a similar benefit by breaking the tempo run into two to four segments. These workouts, also called "cruise intervals," were popularized by exercise physiologist and coach Jack Daniels. For example, three repetitions of 8 minutes each at LT pace, with a 3-minute jog between reps, will provide 24 minutes at LT pace. LT intervals are a good option if you tend to avoid tempo runs. The additional mental effort of tempo runs, however, may pay off when the going gets tough during a race.

LT hills   A great way to increase your lactate threshold is by running long hills. If you are fortunate (or unfortunate) enough to live in an area with a number of good-sized hills, you can do lactate-threshold workouts during a training loop by concentrating on working the hills. For example, suppose you have a 10-mile course that includes four half-mile-long hills and one mile-long hill. If you push the uphills so that you are running at LT intensity, you would accumulate 20 minutes or so at $LT\dot{V}O_2$ during your run.

Adapting to LT Training

In chapter 2, we saw that you can increase your $\dot{V}O_2$max substantially through training. Unfortunately, $\dot{V}O_2$max increases during the first few years of training but then tends to plateau, so if you've been training fairly hard for a number of years, you've probably already

Table 3.4   Examples of Lactate-Threshold Workouts

Tempo runs	20 to 40 minutes at LT pace
LT intervals	4 × 1-mile at LT pace with 2:00 recovery jog 3 × 1 1/2-miles at LT pace with 3:00 recovery jog 2 × 2 1/2-miles at LT pace with 5:00 recovery jog
LT hills	10-mile loop with 3 to 4 miles uphill at LT pace

realized most of your potential gains in $\dot{V}O_2$max. Because $\dot{V}O_2$max plateaus, but lactate threshold continues to increase, adaptations must be occurring inside the muscle cells that allow you to run at a higher percentage of $\dot{V}O_2$max without building up lactic acid. Still, a well-developed $\dot{V}O_2$max is important. In a study comparing elite versus good cyclists, Edward Coyle and colleagues found that 75 percent of the variation in $LT\dot{V}O_2$ is explained by $\dot{V}O_2$max and aerobic enzyme activity (Coyle et al. 1991). $\dot{V}O_2$max sets the upper limit to your $LT\dot{V}O_2$, and aerobic enzyme activity and other factors inside the cells determine how close your $LT\dot{V}O_2$ is to that upper limit.

Studies have shown that the increase in lactate threshold occurs due to both decreased lactate production and increased lactate clearance. The most important of these beneficial changes are (1) increased number and size of mitochondria, (2) increased aerobic enzyme activity, (3) increased capillarization, and (4) increased myoglobin.

Increased number and size of mitochondria   Training at LT pace increases both the number and size of your mitochondria, which are the aerobic-energy-producing factories in your muscle cells. This allows your muscles to produce more energy aerobically, which increases your oxygen consumption at LT, which in turn increases your LT pace.

Increased aerobic enzyme activity   Aerobic enzyme activity represents how much energy is being produced aerobically in the mitochondria. Enzymes speed chemical reactions. By speeding aerobic energy production, you can produce more energy more quickly. Endurance training increases these enzymes, which improves the efficiency of the mitochondria.

Increased capillarization   Capillaries are the smallest blood vessels. Several capillaries typically border each muscle cell. They are the transportation system for the cell, bringing oxygen and fuels in, and sending waste products like carbon dioxide out. Lactate-threshold training increases the number of capillaries per muscle cell, thereby improving the efficiency of delivery and removal, which allows aerobic energy production to be maintained at a high rate.

Increased myoglobin   Myoglobin in your muscle cells serves a similar function to hemoglobin in your blood—it carries oxygen, in this case from the cell membrane to the mitochondria. Lactate-threshold training increases the myoglobin content of your muscle cells, so more oxygen can get to the mitochondria to produce energy.

How You Produce and Use Lactate

Lactate is formed from the incomplete oxidation of carbohydrates. When your body breaks down carbohydrates to produce energy, it forms pyruvate. In your muscle cells, pyruvate is either used to produce energy in the mitochondria or reduced to produce lactic acid. The enzyme that produces lactate and the aerobic enzymes in the mitochondria compete for the available pyruvate.

The key to lactic-acid formation is the rate of pyruvate production relative to the rate of pyruvate use by the mitochondria. The limiting factor is generally whether there are enough aerobic enzymes and oxygen in the mitochondria to use the pyruvate as fast as it is produced. When the rate of glycolysis (which produces pyruvate) is greater than the rate of use of pyruvate by the mitochondria, then lactic acid is formed in the muscles and quickly converted to lactate (the salt of lactic acid). The reduction in pH associated with lactate accumulation in the muscles inactivates enzymes and thereby limits both anaerobic and aerobic energy production.

Blood lactate concentration represents a balance among lactate production by the muscles, diffusion of lactate into the blood, and its consumption by the muscles, heart, liver, and kidneys. You produce and consume lactate even at rest, but as long as production equals consumption, lactate concentration in the blood doesn't rise. The body has several mechanisms for clearing lactate, and the percentage of lactate that follows each pathway varies among rest, exercise, and recovery. Some of the lactate is oxidized within the working muscles, while the rest eventually diffuses out of the muscle and into the blood. After entering the bloodstream, the lactate is primarily either converted to glucose in the liver or used as fuel by the muscles and the heart.

Pure Endurance Training

Distance running is all about endurance. After all, it doesn't matter how much speed you have if you can't cover the distance. In this section, we will consider pure endurance—your ability to keep running.

Defining Pure Endurance

Obviously, the longer the race, the more important endurance becomes, but it's an important attribute for successful racing for all distances from 5K on up. Building pure endurance is the primary determinant of success for novice marathoners (pretty insightful, eh?) and is as important as the lactate threshold for experienced marathoners. If you want to reach your potential in any race of 5K or longer, you should devote a substantial component of your training to pure endurance training.

Improving Pure Endurance

Throughout chapters 2 and 3, we've seen that your body adapts specifically to the stress you place on it. To improve your performance, you should train by simulating the physiological demands of your goal race.

© Ken Lee

Hilly courses provide good venues for lactate threshold workouts.

This principle holds true for pure endurance training. You improve your ability to run long by testing the limits of that ability. By gradually increasing the distance of your longest runs, you provide the greatest stimulus to improve this capacity. How far you should go on your long runs depends on your training history and the distances you plan to race. While inexperienced 5K runners may only need to cover 6 to 8 miles on their long runs, marathoners need to build to long runs of 20 to 23 miles.

Pure endurance training differs from lactate-threshold training in that instead of testing the limits of how fast you can run without accumulating lactate, as on a tempo run, with pure endurance training you're testing the limits of how far you can run without having to slow to a jog. It's important to note that this doesn't mean that the sole purpose of endurance training is covering ground, regardless of pace. Jogging and walking aren't the way to maximize the gains from your long runs. That's because if you do your long runs too slowly, you won't simulate the physiological demands of racing as closely. At the same time, you shouldn't do your long runs as hard as you can because you'll take too long to recover and won't be able to increase your training progressively.

The appropriate intensity for your long runs is in the range of 60 to 80 percent of your heart-rate reserve, which represents about 70 to 85 percent of maximal heart rate. Another way of establishing the appropriate pace for your long runs is to run approximately 0:45 to 1:30 per mile slower than your marathon race pace, or 1:00 to 2:00 per mile slower than your 15K to half-marathon race pace. Running your long runs in this range of intensity will stimulate physiological adaptations, such as increased glycogen storage and fat utilization, without exhausting you to the extent that you take many days to recover.

A good way to go about your long runs is to start out toward the slow end of the range and gradually increase the pace during the run. For example, if you run the marathon at 7:00-per-mile pace, start your long runs at about 8:30 pace and gradually work down to 7:45 pace as the run progresses. It's important to finish your long runs at a strong pace because this is when you're providing the greatest stimulus to increase glycogen storage.

As with the other forms of training, the correct frequency of your long runs depends on your racing goals. The training schedules in

Table 3.5	The Right Way to Do Long Runs for Some Sample Runners		
	Marathon pace	Pace at beginning of long training run	Pace at end of long training run
Runner 1	5:30/mile	7:00/mile	6:15/mile
Runner 2	6:00/mile	7:30/mile	6:45/mile
Runner 3	6:30/mile	8:00/mile	7:15/mile
Runner 4	7:00/mile	8:30/mile	7:45/mile
Runner 5	7:30/mile	9:00/mile	8:15/mile
Runner 6	8:00/mile	9:30/mile	8:45/mile
Runner 7	8:30/mile	10:00/mile	9:15/mile

chapters 6 through 10 emphasize pure endurance training to the appropriate extent for each racing distance. A rule of thumb is to do a high-quality long run two out of every three weeks. That's not to say that you don't do any other endurance-oriented runs during that time, but that you only do high-quality *long* runs in two of every three weeks. That way you'll stay mentally fresh, you'll give your body time to rebuild, and you'll avoid overtraining.

Adapting to Pure Endurance Training

The ways that your muscles adapt to pure endurance training differ in important ways from the adaptations to lactate-threshold training. What happens inside your muscles during those hours-long treks that make them so beneficial?

Increased fat utilization at a given pace   During training and racing, you use a mixture of carbohydrate and fat as fuel. Pure endurance training allows you to use more fat relative to carbohydrate at a given pace. This is a positive adaptation because it allows you to run farther before you run out of glycogen, the storage form of carbohydrate. Running low on glycogen hurts your performance because when this happens you have to rely more on fat. Fat uses oxygen less efficiently than carbohydrate, so when you run low on carbohydrate you have to slow down.

Increased glycogen storage Long runs also teach your muscles to store more glycogen. When your glycogen stores are depleted, your muscles are stimulated to restock to a higher level. This can be viewed as a simple survival mechanism to ensure that you won't run out of glycogen again. By gradually increasing the distance of your long runs, you'll gradually increase your glycogen storage. The faster you run, the more glycogen you burn, so running your long runs at a brisk pace is a more effective way to deplete your glycogen stores (and thereby provide the stimulus for those stores to increase) than running them slowly.

Increased capillary density Long runs increase the number of capillaries per muscle cell, which improves the efficiency of delivery of oxygen and other nutrients, and the removal of carbon dioxide and other waste products. With more capillaries, more oxygen and nutrients can get to your muscle cells. Pure endurance training stimulates this adaptation by providing a sustained requirement for oxygen and other nutrients and for the removal of waste products.

Fiber-type adaptations The higher the percentage of slow-twitch fibers in your muscles, the greater your likelihood of success in the marathon. That's because slow-twitch muscle fibers naturally have more mitochondria, more aerobic enzyme activity, more oxidative capacity, and more capillaries than fast-twitch fibers.

Unfortunately, endurance training hasn't been shown to increase the percentage of slow-twitch fibers in your muscles. This aspect of physiology wasn't recognized by Florence Griffith Joyner and her coaches. After winning the 100-meter and 200-meter dashes at the 1988 Olympics, FloJo announced that she was moving up to the marathon. Had FloJo followed through with her plans, the same physiological characteristics that allowed her to win gold medals in the sprints would have prevented her from succeeding in the marathon. Perhaps this is why FloJo's longest race after announcing herself to be a marathoner was a 20:00 5K. Of course, it would be equally unlikely that Joan Benoit Samuelson would successfully move down to the sprints.

Endurance training, does, however, give your fast-twitch fibers more of the characteristics of slow-twitch fibers. What this means is that although your fast-twitch fibers aren't converted to slow-twitch fibers, they gain a degree of the positive attributes of slow-twitch

Olympic champion Joan Benoit Samuelson devotes much of her training time to boosting her endurance.

fibers. If you were born with a high proportion of fast-twitch fibers, pure endurance training may not make you a champion marathoner, but it will improve your performance.

OK, so now you know how and why to train to improve your $\dot{V}O_2max$, basic speed, lactate threshold, and pure endurance. In chapters 6 through 10, we'll show you the right combination of these types of training for top performance at your chosen distance. But first, let's look at some physiological facts that underlie good training and racing regardless of your distance. In the next chapter, we'll show you how to structure and approach your training to get the most from it. In chapter 5, we'll do the same for race day and the few days before.

CHAPTER 4

Optimal Training

© Ken Lee

The schedules in chapters 6 through 10 are constructed to maximize the benefits you get from your precious training time. Intelligent training, however, is more than, say, doing a good $\dot{V}O_2$max workout and long run most weeks. How you approach your training as a whole, as well as how you live the rest of your life, contributes significantly to how much you benefit from your few key workouts each week.

To that end, this chapter includes physiologically based information that will help you optimize your training. The subjects are diverse yet linked by the idea that they'll help you to train consistently at a high level. Building your mileage with the right base training will help you progress through the race-training schedules. Training by heart rate can help you work at the proper intensity on both hard and easy training days. To get the best results from your training, you must avoid overtraining, perhaps the most common plight of ambitious runners. Combating dehydration helps you run strongly in warm weather as well as recover from one day's training to the next. Avoiding injury allows you to train consistently at a high level. And for women runners, paying attention to how female physiology affects running performance aids in maximizing the benefits of training. Manage these aspects of your training well and you'll be able to race your best.

Base Training

The schedules in chapters 6 through 10 assume that you can comfortably handle the first week's training of whichever schedule you choose to follow. If that's not the case, then the base training schedules that follow will help you bridge the gap between your current training level and the starting point of your goal-race schedules. These 10-week preschedules focus on increasing your mileage, so you'll have the necessary base to complete the first week of your goal-race schedule and progress as your training volume and intensity increase.

You can choose from three schedules. Base A increases your mileage from 15 miles per week to 25 miles per week. This prepares you for cross-country Schedule A-1 and Schedule B of the 5K, 8K-10K, and 15K-half marathon chapters. Base B increases your mileage from 25 miles per week to 40 miles per week. This prepares you for cross-country Schedules A-2, B-1, and B-2, marathon Schedule B, and Schedule C of the 5K and 8K-10K chapters. Base C increases your mileage from 45 miles per week to 60 miles per week. This prepares you for Schedule C of the 15K-half marathon and marathon chapters.

Base Training Schedule
Base A: Build to 25 miles/week

Weeks before schedule	LR1	LR2	Lactate threshold workouts	Basic speed	Week's mileage
10	4	4	–	–	15
9	5	4	–	–	16
8	5	4	–	–	17
7	5	5	–	–	18
6	6	5	–	–	19
5	6	5	–	–	20
4	6	6	–	8 × 100 meters	21
3	7	6	2 × 1-mile LT intervals	–	22
2	7	6	–	8 × 100 meters	23
1	8	6	2 × 1 1/2-mile LT intervals	–	25

Base Training Schedule
Base B: Build to 40 miles/week

Weeks before schedule	LR1	LR2	Lactate threshold workouts	Basic speed	Week's mileage
10	6	5	–	–	25
9	7	6	–	–	27
8	7	6	–	–	29
7	7	6	–	–	30
6	8	7	–	8 × 100 meters	32
5	8	7	–	–	34
4	9	8	–	8 × 100 meters	36
3	9	8	2 × 1 1/2-mile LT intervals	–	37
2	10	8	–	8 × 100 meters	38
1	10	8	2 × 1 1/2-mile LT intervals	–	25

Base Training Schedule
Base C: Build to 60 miles/week

Weeks before schedule	LR1	LR2	Lactate threshold workouts	Basic speed	Week's mileage
10	11	9	–	8 × 100 meters	45
9	12	9	–	–	47
8	12	9	–	8 × 100 meters	49
7	12	10	–	–	50
6	13	10	–	8 × 100 meters	52
5	13	11	2 × 1 1/2 mile LT intervals	–	54
4	13	11	–	8 × 100 meters	56
3	14	11	2 × 1 1/2-mile LT intervals	–	57
2	14	11	2 3 2 mile LT intervals		58
1	15	11	2 × 1 1/2-mile LT intervals	–	60

Schedules Explained

The base training schedules are 10 weeks long, which is an appropriate time in which to build up your mileage. We include lactate-threshold workouts in each base schedule as LT intervals to start the adaptation process and prepare you to begin the schedules in chapters 6 through 10. Basic speed sessions in these schedules will help you maintain your speed during this time. During base training, when nearly all your running is easy mileage, you may feel slow and sluggish. This makes it tough when it's time to start the faster running of $\dot{V}O_2max$ workouts. The 8 × 100-meter basic speed sessions of the base schedules will prepare you for the more difficult sessions in the schedules in chapters 6 through 10.

Longest run   This is simply the longest run for the week. The schedules gradually increase your longest run to help prepare you for the long runs in the schedules in chapters 6 through 10. For runners building to 60 miles per week, the long run starts at 11 miles and increases to 15 miles. For runners building to 25 miles per week, the long run starts at 4 miles and increases to 8 miles. See chapter 3 for more on long runs.

Second longest run   This is the second longest run for the week. The purpose of these sessions is to reinforce the training adaptations of the long runs. These runs increase in distance in a similar pattern to the long runs. You should run the second longest run at a pace similar to or slightly faster than the long run. If your races will be on hilly terrain, try to simulate race conditions in selecting where to do these runs.

Lactate-threshold workouts   We have designed the workouts in this column to increase your lactate threshold. LT intervals, run at your lactate-threshold pace, are explained in detail in chapter 3. Lactate-threshold pace is approximately your 15K to half-marathon race pace. (For other ways to estimate lactate-threshold pace, see chapter 3.) For these workouts, warm up for about two miles, run the LT intervals, and then cool down for a mile or two. You should run easily for two to five minutes between your LT intervals.

Basic speed   These short accelerations up to full speed are explained in detail in chapter 2. As noted earlier, these workouts will help maintain your leg turnover when you start the schedules in chapters 6 through 10.

Putting it all together   As an example of how to structure the week's training, look at three weeks to go in Base Schedule B (building to 40 miles per week). The schedule for that week includes four workouts. Add easy recovery runs or cross-training as necessary to reach the total of 37 miles for the week (see table 4.1). (For how to equate cross-training with running mileage, see the injury prevention section of this chapter.)

Managing the many aspects of your training allows you to get the most from your hard work.

Table 4.1	Properly Structuring a Sample Week From Base Schedule B
Sunday	9 miles
Monday	Off
Tuesday	7 miles
Wednesday	LT intervals (7 miles, including warm-up, 2 × 1 1/2-miles at LT pace, and cool-down)
Thursday	8 miles
Friday	Off
Saturday	6 miles
Mileage for week	37

A typical way to complete this week's training is to do the longest run on Sunday and take Monday off. Tuesday could be the third longest run. Wednesday would be time for the hardest session, the LT intervals. Thursday could be the second longest run, followed by a day off on Friday and a 6-mile run on Saturday. You complete the 37 miles with five days of running, with the workouts evenly spaced throughout the week.

Using Heart Rate to Monitor Your Training

During exercise, your heart rate provides valuable information on your training intensity because it reflects how hard your heart is working. Heart monitors are the best way to measure your heart rate while running—they're accurate and they allow you to check your heart rate without having to stop. Most runners can't get an accurate exercise heart rate by taking their pulse. It's easy to miscount beats, and your heart rate slows quickly when you stop to take your pulse.

You can base your training on a percentage of your maximum heart rate or on a percentage of your heart-rate reserve. Although heart-rate reserve is more accurate for monitoring your training, it involves a little more calculation, so let's look at both methods.

Your heart-rate reserve is your maximal heart rate minus your resting heart rate. Heart-rate reserve estimates the percentage of your $\dot{V}O_2$max at which you're working. It shows how much your heart rate can increase with exercise and therefore represents the intensity of training. For example, let's say Ed's maximal heart rate is 190 and his resting heart rate is 50; his heart-rate reserve, then, is 140.

To calculate heart-rate reserve, you first need to determine your maximal heart rate. Several formulas based on age are available for doing this, all of which are fairly inaccurate because there's such a wide range of maximal heart rates for a person of a given age. These formulas will tell you only the average maximum heart rate for someone of your age; your actual maximal heart rate may be as much as 20 beats above or below this average. Therefore, if you base your training on these formulas but are above or below the average, you'll be training too easy or too hard. In both cases, you'll be far from maximizing your potential.

Fortunately, it's not difficult to find your actual maximal heart rate. Do a good warm-up followed by several accelerations up to sprint speed. After you have warmed up thoroughly, run very hard for 2 minutes while wearing a heart monitor. If you run as hard as you can, you'll most likely be within two to three beats of your maximal heart rate by the end of the run. If you aren't sure whether you gave an all-out effort, jog for 10 minutes and repeat the test. Some runners find they get a slightly higher heart rate if they perform this test uphill.

Now that you know your maximal heart rate, subtract your resting heart rate to determine your heart-rate reserve. Your resting heart rate is your heart rate when you first wake in the morning, before you get out of bed. Take your pulse over a few days, and you'll likely find an average resting heart rate. If you use an alarm during the week, wait until you have a few days when you can wake naturally to check your pulse.

Calculating Heart-Rate Reserve

Heart-rate reserve (HRR) = maximal heart rate − resting heart rate

Target heart rate = resting heart rate + appropriate percentage of HRR

Table 4.2 shows the proper heart-rate intensity for the types of training detailed in this book, both for training by heart-rate reserve and by maximal heart rate. As an example, let's say that Ed wants to do a workout at his $\dot{V}O_2$max training pace, which is about 95 percent of $\dot{V}O_2$max. We multiply 95 percent by Ed's heart-rate reserve of 140 beats per minute and then add his resting heart rate of 50 to get a target heart rate of 183 beats per minute. Ed would then run hard enough to get his heart rate up to about 183 beats per minute during his intervals. It may take a minute or so for heart rate to increase to that level, so don't be concerned if your heart rate is lower than the target at the beginning of an interval.

Alternatively, let's say that Ed wants to base his training on maximal heart rate rather than heart-rate reserve. Ed does a recovery run, keeping his heart rate below 75 percent of his max. With a max of 190, Ed would therefore multiply 190 by 75 percent to get 142. He would then run easy enough to keep his heart rate below this ceiling for the duration of his run.

Note that heart rate is affected by factors other than running speed. Caffeine increases heart rate, as do dehydration and running in the heat. For example, if you're running a workout on a warm day, your heart rate will tend to increase several beats per minute as the workout progresses. Your heart rate increases because (a) your blood volume decreases as you sweat, which decreases your stroke volume, so your heart must beat faster to pump the same amount of blood and (b) more of your blood is sent to the skin for evaporative cooling when you run in the heat, which leaves less blood going to the working muscles, so heart rate must increase to supply enough oxygen to the muscles.

Table 4.2   Target Heart-Rate Training Intensities

Training type	Percent $\dot{V}O_2$max	Percent HRR	Percent max heart rate
Speed	Faster than $\dot{V}O_2$max pace	Not used	Not used
$\dot{V}O_2$max	95-100	95-98	95-98
Lactate threshold	75-90	75-90	80-92
Endurance	65-80	65-80	75-85
Recovery	< 70	< 70	< 75

© Ken Lee

In warm weather, your heart rate will be higher at a given pace than on cool days.

How should you account for this upward drift in heart rate on hot days? First, you can reduce it by drinking enough before and during your run. If you stay properly hydrated, your heart rate will still go up some owing to heat, but not as much as if you don't drink. (We'll say more about battling dehydration later in this chapter.) In hot weather, of course, it's nearly impossible to take in enough fluid to compensate for sweating, especially if you're running hard. On those days, acknowledge that your heart rate at a given pace will be higher than usual. Allow for an increase of 5 beats per minute; for example, if Ed's recovery run is on a 90-degree day, he could set 147, rather than

142, as his ceiling. After that 5-beat allowance, though, slow your pace if that's what it takes to stay within your adjusted range.

Overcoming Overtraining

Woke up. Got out of bed.

Oh my God, do I feel dead.

Then I went outside and tried to run.

Somethin' feels broke, and I hope it's just a dream.

—"A Day in the Life of the Overtrained Runner"
(with apologies to the Beatles)

Have you ever woken up with your legs feeling heavy, your mind wondering how you're ever going to find the energy to go for a run? Sure you have—every distance runner has. After all, fatigue is the point of training; it provides the stimulus for the body to reach new levels of fitness. There's a threshold, however, beyond which the stimulus overwhelms your ability to recover, and you enter the domain of overtraining.

Defining Overtraining

Put broadly, overtraining is the result of working out hard more frequently than your body can handle. Adapting positively to training takes place when more buildup (anabolism) than breakdown (catabolism) occurs in muscle-cell protein, mitochondrial protein, aerobic enzymes, and other desired reactions to exercise. When you're overtraining, however, the opposite occurs—your ability to recover is outpaced by the stresses that you're subjecting your body to, leading to decreased performance.

That said, it's important to distinguish overtraining from mere lingering fatigue. Many runners have been led to believe that all fatigue is harmful and that its occurrence is a sign of overtraining. Most running publications offer a vaguely defined concept of overtraining and a subsequent call for drastically reduced mileage as an all-purpose diagnosis and cure for any admission of fatigue. Often, people are told that they're overtrained simply when they're temporarily tired from increasing their mileage. In these cases, cutting your mileage and intensity for a few days usually returns you to your normal energy and performance levels.

It's more useful to see overtraining as a chronic condition resulting from too much high-intensity training. Although the causes of over-training aren't well understood, many cases are believed to be due to overstimulation of the sympathetic nervous system. The sympathetic nervous system is your body's mechanism for regulating your reaction to stress; it causes increased levels of adrenaline in the blood, as well as elevated heart rate, blood pressure, breathing rate, and other reactions that prepare you for fight or flight. It does so not only in response to a sudden crisis but also in reaction to more drawn-out episodes, such as twice-weekly interval sessions coupled with weekly races.

Your sympathetic nervous system responds to all the stresses in your life—training, sleep deprivation, nutritional deficits, job woes, family and personal relationship struggles, and so forth. When the amount of stress in your life is under control, you can deal with a stressful situation—on the track, at the office, in the home—and then relax and recover enough to handle the next round. But constant sympathetic stimulation leads to the feeling that your mind and body are always engaged; your fight-or-flight response is always activated, meaning that it's controlling you rather than the other way around. As a result, you're simultaneously "on" and fatigued, and therefore unable to relax fully or perform at your best.

Identifying Overtraining

The symptoms of overtraining vary among runners. Symptoms often reported include trouble sleeping, frequent colds, increased resting heart rate, weight loss, impaired racing and training times, slow recovery from training, and a loss of enthusiasm for running (and most other things). Under normal training loads, running has small, short-term effects on immune function, but overtraining can lead to general immune system suppression, resulting in increased susceptibility to infections and decreased ability to fight off infections. In female athletes, over-training may also be associated with amenorrhea. You may have any combination of these symptoms, as well as others.

There's no foolproof test for identifying overtraining. The balance between testosterone and cortisol is thought to determine the ability to adapt positively to training. This ratio has been used as an indicator of overtraining because overtraining can lead to

© Human Kinetics

The effects aren't usually this dramatic, but overtraining always leads to less-than-optimal performance.

decreased levels of testosterone and increased levels of cortisol in the blood. Most runners, of course, don't know their normal testosterone and cortisol levels, nor do they have the means to measure them frequently, making this method more interesting than helpful in determining why you haven't been racing up to par lately.

The two most common methods of identifying overtraining measure heart rate, either first thing in the morning or while running at a set pace. If you take your pulse when you wake each morning, then after a few days you'll know your normal resting heart rate (if you're not overtrained when you start doing so). An increase of more than five beats per minute above normal indicates overtraining. Unfortunately, this test isn't reliable if you wake with an alarm.

Similarly, you can evaluate overtraining by measuring your heart rate while running at a given speed. If your heart rate increases more than 4 to 5 percent, then you should take it easy for a few days. For example, if your heart rate at 7:00-per-mile pace is typically 150 beats per minute, but lately it's closer to 160 on most days, that's evidence that you should back off. Be aware, though, that heart rate can also increase because of caffeine consumption, dehydration, and heat and humidity, so you can make accurate comparisons only under similar conditions.

Accurately identifying overtraining is further made difficult by the fact that the above conditions are often caused by less-severe factors. As we've already noted, sudden increases in volume can, in the short term, lead to the same symptoms of lethargy and decreased performance. So can poor sleep, dehydration, and inadequate glycogen intake. When you hit a spell of decreased performance, look first to these factors as explanations. During a three- to five-day period, try these steps: Drink enough so that your urine is consistently clear in color. Make sure that you take in 60 to 70 percent of your calories as carbohydrate and that you're getting adequate protein. Look at your training log for recent increases in mileage or high-intensity workouts. If three to five days of low mileage at an easy pace, combined with adequate carbohydrate intake, water, and sleep, don't eliminate your fatigue, and you have no other signs of illness, then you're probably overtrained.

Recovering From Overtraining

To recover from overtraining, you need to reestablish a positive balance between buildup and breakdown. You can accomplish this only by (shudder) reducing your training. Training intensity is more important than training volume in recovering from over- training, so cut back more on speedwork than on distance. How long it takes to recover depends on how deep a hole you have dug. You can usually remedy overtraining in 10 to 14 days. Long-term overtraining syndrome or staleness, however, may require several months for full recovery. Fortunately, long-term overtraining syn- drome is relatively rare and usually is related to additional stresses, such as eating disorders or anemia. If you take it easy for two weeks and don't feel appreciably better, then you should see a physician who specializes in working with athletes for a thorough checkup.

Besides altering your training, you may need to modify your lifestyle. If chronic glycogen depletion led to your lethargy, pay attention to your carbohydrate intake or see a nutritionist. If you have been constantly dehydrated, then devise strategies for staying fully hydrated, such as keeping a two-liter bottle of water at your desk. And if sleep deprivation is impairing your ability to recover, then do your best to eliminate the deficit. (You could also quit your job, but that would only exchange one set of stresses for another.)

Preventing Overtraining

Overtraining is an individual phenomenon. Your genetics, your level of fitness, and the sum of stresses in your life determine the training load you can handle. What's normal for you may represent overtraining for your running partner. Effective training relies on managing your body's ability to recover and adapt. Overtraining simply represents poor management. You can train exceptionally hard and not become overtrained as long as you allow time between hard workouts to let your body recover.

The best way to prevent overtraining is to know thyself. Pay attention to your body's signals—learn how much carbohydrate, protein, water, and sleep you need. Keep a thorough training log so that you can learn from your previous responses to training. Learn your individual training or stress threshold so that you avoid exceeding your body's ability to adapt.

Avoiding Dehydration

Running in heat and humidity can quickly lead to dehydration, which ranks with Dobermans and drivers among runners' worst enemies. Dehydration hurts your performance in two ways—it causes you to slow during a given run, and it slows your ability to recover for the next workout. In extreme cases, continuing to run when dehydrated can lead to heat stroke and death.

To understand better the dangers of dehydration, consider what happens when you run on a warm day. First, your body sends more blood to the skin for evaporative cooling, leaving less oxygen-rich blood going to your leg muscles. Second, the warmer it is, the more you sweat and the more your blood volume decreases. Less blood returns to your heart, so it pumps less blood per contraction. Your heart rate, therefore, must increase to pump the same amount of blood. The result is that you can't maintain as fast a pace.

It's not unusual to lose 3 to 4 pounds of water per hour when running on a warm day. At this rate, after two hours, a 150-pound runner would lose 6 to 8 pounds, representing a 4 to 5 percent loss in body weight. How significant a loss is that? In one study, exercise physiologist and marathoner Larry Armstrong, induced dehydration equal to 2 percent of body weight and observed a 6 percent decrease in speed over 5K or 10K. That's a 3 percent decline in performance for each 1 percent decrease in body weight caused by dehydration. After losing 4 to 5 percent of his body weight, then, our 150-pound runner could expect a 10 to 15 percent decrease in performance; that's about an extra minute per mile. Losing more than 4 to 5 percent of your body weight can induce heatstroke, in which case slowing by a minute per mile will be among your least concerns.

Runners must also consider dehydration's cumulative effect. During the hottest times of the year, runners are often unaware that they're constantly dehydrated. But if you replace even a little less fluid than you lose each day, then after a few days you'll start to run poorly without knowing why. Let's say that during a hot week, our 150-pound runner fails to rehydrate himself fully each day and by the end of the week has a cumulative loss of 2 pounds. His weight will have decreased by more than 1 percent, and according to Armstrong's study he can expect his performance to decrease by 3 percent.

Preventing Dehydration

If you're running in temperatures above 70 degrees, or above 60 degrees with high humidity, staying properly hydrated can become a challenge. You need a strategy for preventing dehydration during today's run and for minimizing the cumulative effects of hot-weather running.

Before workouts and races, concentrate on drinking enough water to ensure that you're fully hydrated. Don't rely just on your thirst. Your body's thirst mechanism is imperfect—by the time you're thirsty, you're partly dehydrated. Drink enough so that your urine is frequent and clear in color. Also, drink small amounts throughout the day rather than a large amount a few times. It takes time for your body tissues to absorb water, so you can't just drink half a gallon of fluid in one sitting and assume that you're fully hydrated. To top off the tank, the American College of Sports Medicine recommends drinking about half a liter of fluid about two hours before exercise to help ensure adequate hydration and allow time to excrete excess water.

How much you should drink during your runs depends on the heat and humidity, and how far you're running. The maximum amount you should drink is the amount that can empty from your stomach. Research has shown that most runners' stomachs can

© Victah

Staying hydrated improves your performance in warm weather.

empty only six to seven ounces of fluid every 15 minutes during running. If you drink more than that, the extra fluid will slosh around in your stomach and provide no benefit. You may be able to handle more or less than the average, however, so experiment with how much liquid your stomach will tolerate.

Can you take in enough fluid to prevent dehydration on a hot day? On the hottest days, you may lose four to five pounds of water an hour. We already estimated that your stomach can absorb about 28 ounces, or a little less than two pounds, per hour. That leaves a deficit of two to three pounds per hour. You can't absorb enough to keep up, so the farther you run, the greater your fluid deficit will be.

The solution is to be flexible with your training schedule. Run at the time of day when the weather is the least taxing on the body and be prepared to face the physiological facts. On a hot, humid day, slow your pace from the outset rather than wait until your body forces you to slow.

To prevent cumulative dehydration, weigh yourself before and after running, calculate how much weight you lost, and then drink with the objective of bringing your weight back to normal. Your blood and other fluids help to remove waste products and bring nutrients to tissues for repair, so replacing lost fluids quickly after running will speed your recovery.

What to Drink

There are two excellent options for preventing dehydration and for rehydrating after a workout—water and carbohydrate replacement drinks. Nothing beats water for pure hydration. The advantage of replacement drinks that contain 4 to 6 percent carbohydrate is that they provide energy and are absorbed as quickly as water. The carbohydrates can help your performance during workouts or races lasting longer than an hour.

Avoid caffeinated drinks, such as coffee, tea, and colas, because caffeine is a diuretic—it causes you to urinate more frequently. Drinking caffeinated beverages adds to, rather than helps with, dehydration. Similarly, beer and other alcoholic beverages may help calm your nerves but are counterproductive to hydration because alcohol is a diuretic. If you drink caffeinated drinks or alcohol, drink at least an equal amount of water to balance the dehydrating effect. For example, if you have two beers with dinner, drink at least an extra 24 ounces of water.

Injury Prevention

Successful distance running requires discipline. You must have the mind-set to run day after day, despite the vagaries of the weather and the frequent intrusions of other aspects of your life. Too often, however, in the pursuit of excellence, injuries intervene and lead many runners to abandon their lofty goals. Yet because injuries are usually predictable, you can often prevent their occurrence.

In most of this book, we focus on how to improve your cardiovascular system and your muscles' ability to perform metabolically. For you to run to your potential, however, your muscles must also be able to perform mechanically. When you run, your bones, muscles, tendons, and ligaments deal with forces of three to five times your body weight with each step. To continue running, your tissues must be able to withstand these loads even when they're repeated thousands of times per day. An injury is a failure of your body to handle these repetitive forces.

What causes muscle strains, tendinitis, ligament damage, and stress fractures? The forces to which you subject your body parts are either too high or repeated too many times. In other words, injuries occur because of too much impact shock per step or the cumulative effect of too many steps. Most running injuries occur because of the repetitive nature of the running stride. You can prevent many running injuries by eliminating the root causes. You can do this in two ways—by increasing the ability of your tissues to tolerate a force repeatedly and by decreasing the cumulative amount of force. You can address the former by improving your flexibility and correcting muscle imbalances and the latter by adjusting your running surface, terrain, shoes, and mileage.

Improving Flexibility With Stretching

Watch an animal run and you'll notice that running is a flowing movement that involves the whole body. For example, when a horse gallops, you can see the interaction of its feet, legs, back, neck, and head. This coordination makes galloping an economical way to cover ground. Similarly, your body moves most economically when your whole body works in synch. A tight neck and shoulders will affect your running as surely as tight hamstrings. To flow well, you must be flexible. You can improve your flexibility with stretching and yoga.

Stretching increases the length of muscle and connective tissue and thereby reduces muscle tension and helps to prevent injuries. Every runner knows about stretching, yet many runners stretch incorrectly. A typical routine is to stretch quickly and forcefully for a few minutes, then head out for a run. That type of stretching isn't effective in preventing injuries. Aggressive stretching can overstretch muscles and cause muscle strains. To be effective, stretching must be done correctly.

The best time to stretch is before your workout but after a warmup. The warm-up increases blood flow to the muscles, thereby

© Victah

Stretching before workouts and races tends to make you feel better during your run.

increasing their ability to stretch without injury. Preworkout stretching not only helps prevent injuries but also tends to make you feel better during the workout. Stretching after the workout helps your muscles and connective tissue maintain their length until the next workout.

You need not restrict your stretching to before and after running, when you may not have the time or inclination to do a complete stretching session. In that case, you'll benefit by fitting in stretching during other times of the day, such as when watching television.

The key to improving your flexibility is to stretch consistently at a comfortable level, not aggressively for a few minutes a few times per week. Each stretch should be gentle and prolonged. It's often helpful to time your stretches. Hold stretches for a minimum of 15 seconds and preferably for at least 30 seconds. If you find it difficult to stretch for 30 seconds, it may be because you hold your breath when stretching. An athlete who holds her breath while stretching generally releases the stretch after 10 to 15 seconds, when she needs to breathe. You should always be able to breathe while stretching.

After stretching a muscle group, let it relax for the same amount of time that you held the stretch, then repeat the stretch a second time. Unlike your hard training sessions, stretching isn't supposed to test your limits. If you stretch too quickly or bounce when stretching, a protective reflex is activated. This reflex, which prevents the muscle from tearing, increases rather than reduces the tension in your muscles.

Two good books about stretching are *Sport Stretch*, by Michael Alter, and *Stretching*, by Bob and Jean Anderson.

Correcting Muscle Imbalances

Many injuries are caused by simple mechanical problems stemming from muscle imbalances. If you take time off from running, most injuries go away. But if muscle imbalance caused your injury, the problem will eventually reappear when you resume training. Unfortunately, it's usually not possible to assess muscle imbalances on your own. If you start to develop pain when running, a physical therapist can test the strength of your muscles and determine whether a muscle imbalance is causing your problem.

For example, pain under the kneecap is often related to an imbalance within the quadriceps muscles on the front of the thigh. Your quads consist of four muscles, each of which exerts forces on your kneecap. All of these muscles pull upward, but two pull toward the outside of your leg, and the other two pull toward the inside. Problems arise when the two muscles that pull toward the inside exert too little force; the kneecap is pulled toward the outside of the leg and becomes irritated. To correct this problem, you need to strengthen the two quadriceps muscles that pull toward the inside. You can accomplish this by doing resistance exercises, such as putting a pillow between your legs and squeezing your thighs together or doing straight-leg raises with your thigh externally rotated.

Muscle imbalances are often related to poor flexibility in other body parts. For example, lower-back problems are common among runners because of a combination of tight hamstrings and weak abdominal muscles.

Muscle imbalances tend to develop over time. By identifying a muscle imbalance when pain first develops, you can correct it before it results in a full-fledged injury.

Yoga for a Balanced Body

Yoga improves flexibility, posture, and coordination, and develops strength. It's also relaxing and therapeutic. Unfortunately, yoga is generally misunderstood in the United States. Yoga is a physically demanding series of poses that improves strength and flexibility while reducing stress. Although some forms of yoga involve meditation, the physical benefits alone are well worth the effort involved.

"Yoga" means "union." A yoga session consists of a series of poses that uses the whole body. Unlike stretching, which tends to isolate one muscle at a time, yoga works several muscle groups simultaneously. For example, the classic position called downward dog works the muscles of the arms, shoulders, back, hips, legs, and feet. The various yoga positions include standing poses, seated poses, forward bends, and inverted poses.

Breathing correctly is an integral part of yoga. Correct breathing can lead to greater improvements in flexibility and a deeper sense of relaxation. Yoga can help you to reduce the overall stress in your life. To start, look for an experienced instructor in your area or buy a yoga video. A good book for runners on the subject is *Power Yoga*, by Beryl Bender Birch. By strengthening and stretching muscles in a balanced way, yoga is one of the few ways to prevent the problems that lead to injuries. As your body becomes stronger and more flexible, you'll find yourself looking forward to yoga positions that you initially found challenging and difficult.

Improving Muscle Resiliency With Massage

Muscle injuries occur when muscle fibers are stressed before they're ready to work hard again. Whether overworked muscle fibers develop spasms and strains depends on your approach to recovery. If you're patient enough to allow this damage to the muscle to repair itself before your next hard workout, then you probably don't need massage. If, however, you're like most runners, you usually ignore complaining muscles.

Sports massage can speed the recovery process. Although there are many types of massage, sports massage is designed to return overworked muscles to prime readiness to train again. Sports massage isn't gentle—it consists of deep muscle work. Few things are as beneficial for training as a deep massage. Running legend Bill Rodgers has gotten a weekly massage since 1980. He credits this habit with allowing him to train and race hard for nearly three decades with only one serious injury.

Fortunately, if you can't get a regular massage, you can receive many of the benefits through self-massage. You can easily reach your hamstrings, quadriceps, calf muscles, and feet, and with some hard work can relieve muscle tightness before injuries develop. Self-massage devices, such as the Stick, are beneficial here.

Preventing Injuries by Minimizing Impact Shock

So far, we've focused on how to improve your body's ability to deal with the impact shock of running. Now let's look at ways to decrease the forces that your body must absorb. One solution, of course, is simply to stop running. Injured runners frequently receive this advice. Fortunately, there are less drastic solutions.

Keeping your shoes in good condition can make a big difference in the amount of shock that your body absorbs. The cushioning properties of all running shoes currently on the market break down substantially after less than 800 miles of running. For runners training 20 miles per week, this represents 40 weeks of use. The 100-mile-a-week crowd reaches 800 miles in only 8 weeks. Depending on your size, running mechanics, and the shoes you wear, you may need to replace your running shoes after as little as 400 miles.

It's also a good idea to use different pairs of running shoes on different days. The forces your body must deal with vary somewhat in different pairs of shoes. By switching shoes, you'll make the shock that your feet, legs, and back receive somewhat less repetitive. This reduction in the repetitiveness of the forces may thwart the development of an injury.

The surface that you run on also makes a large difference in the amount of pounding absorbed by your body. Concrete is the least forgiving surface for running—shin splints and stress fractures incurred on concrete may have been prevented by running on

© Stacey Cramp

Although convenient and ubiquitous, blacktop is less than an ideal running surface.

another surface. Blacktop, while softer than concrete, is far from an ideal running surface. (Our bodies didn't evolve while running on blacktop.) Search for natural surfaces—dirt paths, grass fields, golf courses, trails, anywhere that will allow you to run with less shock and less chance of injury. The higher the percentage of your training that you do off-road, the lower your likelihood of developing overuse injuries. The one injury that interrupted Bill Rodgers's career came when he switched from doing most of his running on grass to asphalt.

If you feel that you're on the verge of an injury, avoid downhill running. The impact forces of downhill running are significantly greater than for level running, so by avoiding downhills you may prevent an injury from occurring.

Cross-Training Option

Cross-training allows you to maintain your cardiovascular fitness without adding to the number of times that your feet strike the ground. Cycling, rowing, swimming, running in water, in-line skating, cross-country skiing, stair climbing, slideboarding, arm cranking, and other options are available for working out without the impact of running. Unfortunately, no cross-training method accurately simulates running. Running is running, cycling is cycling, and so forth. Because your muscles adapt specifically to the type of training you do, the closest substitute to running is running in water with a flotation vest. Because you make no contact with the ground, however, even water running doesn't come close to replicating the muscular demands of running on land.

Although your conversions won't be perfect, you can roughly translate the cardiovascular benefits of various forms of cross-training to running using heart rate. The relationship between your heart rate and how hard you're working is similar for running, cycling, in-line skating, cross-country skiing, rowing, slideboarding, or stair climbing. For example, if you want to keep your heart rate between 130 and 140 beats per minute during recovery training, the physiological effects of these types of cross-training will be similar to running. The relationship doesn't work as well when running in water or swimming because of the pressure of the water around your body. The heart rate-effort relationship is also different for swimming because of that sport's horizontal body position. During both swimming and running in water, your heart rate will be lower than during running.

Cross-training is an excellent option for recovery training. You improve the recovery process by pumping blood to the muscles without adding to the cumulative pounding on tissues. Among world-class runners, who are usually obedient to the weekly mileage gods, are a growing minority who cross train on their recovery days. For example, Joan Nesbit swims and water runs to supplement her regular running. She credits this approach with allowing her to remain uninjured and make the 1996 U.S. Olympic team at 10,000 meters. The race-training schedules in chapters 6 through 10 encourage cross-training on recovery days if you tend to become injured above a certain level of weekly running mileage.

Physiological Considerations for Female Runners

Although women have typically been discouraged from training at the same volume and intensity as men, there's little, if any, physiological basis to justify this practice. The physiology of running is the same for both genders—studies have shown that women obtain the same percentage increase in $\dot{V}O_2$max with training as men and that the overall pattern of adaptations to training is identical in men and women runners.

Still, physiology puts women at a disadvantage when competing against men, from the 100-meter dash to the marathon, and at every distance between. Among the gender-related physiological differences that affect running performance are the following:

1. Women have smaller hearts than men, so the heart pumps less blood per contraction, resulting in a higher heart rate at a given workload.

2. Women have lower hemoglobin levels than men, so less oxygen can be transported to the working muscles.

3. Women have higher essential body-fat stores than men.

4. Women have less total muscle mass than men because of lower levels of testosterone.

For distance runners, one of the main effects of these factors is that women have lower $\dot{V}O_2$max values than men. Although yet to be proven, there's reason to think that beyond the marathon, these factors might not be as much of a disadvantage. In ultramarathons, there's speculation that women may be capable of equal or better performances than men because of a greater ability to use fat for fuel and the advantage of smaller body size in dissipating heat.

Three Influences on Performance

Three other issues unique to women's physiology can affect running performance. First is the menstrual cycle. The effect of menstrual cycles on running varies widely among women. Studies investigating the effects of the menstrual cycle on athletic performance have been inconclusive, in large part because of this variability. While some women experience little change in performance during their cycles, others find that their athletic abilities are highly sensitive to the phases of the menstrual cycle. For the latter women, decreased performance occurs most often during the premenstrual and early flow phases of the cycle.

© Victah

A woman's best race results come from a training plan that considers unique factors in female physiology.

What you care most about, of course, is how your monthly cycle affects you. This is one more area in which each runner is an experiment of one. The only way to find the impact of your menstrual cycle on running performance is through personal experience. In your training log, track how your cycle affects your performance, then plan accordingly. If, for example, you note that your energy level is often lower during your premenstrual phase, allow for greater fatigue in your workouts and try not to schedule important races during this time.

Another issue is how oral contraceptives affect running performance. Oddly, oral contraceptives have been observed to work both positively and negatively. For women who have decreased performance during the premenstrual or flow stages of their cycles, oral contraceptives can boost performance by eliminating these phases. Some women, however, experience negative side effects from birth-control pills that can reduce performance, including weight gain, fatigue, nausea, and hypertension.

Because both the fluctuations in performance during the menstrual cycle and the extent of side effects from use of oral contraceptives vary substantially among women, it's impossible to predict confidently the impact of birth-control pills on your performance. Each premenopausal woman runner must evaluate the pros and cons and determine whether to use birth-control pills based on her experience.

Finally, women runners need to be more careful than men runners about preventing low iron stores. Iron is a component of hemoglobin in your red blood cells. Hemoglobin carries oxygen from your lungs to your muscles. If your hemoglobin level is low, therefore, less oxygen reaches your muscles, and your $\dot{V}O_2max$ and racing performances suffer. In addition, iron is a component of many other substances in your body, such as enzymes in your muscle cells for aerobic energy production.

For premenopausal women runners, maintaining normal iron levels is often a challenge. Besides menstrual blood loss, women runners' iron levels tend to be low because of low iron intake, foot-strike hemolysis (breakdown of red blood cells when your foot strikes the ground), increased blood volume from training, iron loss through sweat and urine, and iron loss through the gastrointestinal system. Sedentary premenopausal women need about 15 milligrams of iron per day, compared to 10 milligrams per day for men and postmenopausal women. Specific iron requirements for high-mileage runners haven't been established.

If you have low iron, you may feel that you're frequently dragging—your heart rate may be elevated while your enthusiasm for running has sunk. A blood test will confirm whether you're suffering from low iron. Find out both your hemoglobin and serum ferritin levels. Normal hemoglobin concentration for women ranges from 12 to 16 grams per 100 milliliters of blood; for an endurance athlete, the lower end of normal should be extended by about 1 gram per 100 milliliters because of increased blood volume. Ferritin is a measure of your body's iron stores. Although normal reference ferritin levels for women are 10 to 200 nanograms per milliliter, some physiologists believe that performance is affected when ferritin falls below 25 nanograms per milliliter.

As with other running problems, such as injuries, the best strategy is to avoid low iron in the first place. Good food sources of iron include liver, lean meat, oysters, egg yolk, dark green leafy vegetables, legumes, dried fruit, and whole grain or enriched cereals and bread. E. Randy Eichner, chief of hematology at the University of Oklahoma Health Sciences Center, offers these tips to prevent iron deficiency:

1. Eat three ounces of lean red meat or dark poultry a couple of times each week.
2. Don't drink coffee or tea with meals because they reduce iron absorption.
3. Eat or drink vitamin C-rich foods with meals to increase iron absorption.
4. Use cast-iron cookware, particularly for acidic foods like spaghetti sauce.

Although these recommendations may seem like subtle changes in diet, they can affect your iron levels. For example, you'll absorb three times as much iron from your cereal and toast if you switch from coffee to orange juice with breakfast. If you are currently iron deficient or have a history of low iron, then iron supplements may be necessary along with dietary changes. In that case, you should seek advice from a sports nutritionist or doctor who has experience with endurance athletes. As with any mineral, too much iron can be a health hazard.

When you're careful about the topics that we've discussed in this chapter, you can get the most out of your training. But there's more than that to reaching your potential in races. In the next chapter, we'll look at what you can do just before and during races to maximize your performance.

CHAPTER 5

Optimal Racing

© Victah

In the last chapter, we looked at ways to get the most from your training. After this chapter, the schedules in chapters 6 through 10 will get you to the starting line of your goal race with the appropriate blend of speed and endurance. Still, it's possible to jeopardize months of good training with simple mistakes in the few days before the race or during the race. Paying attention to what might seem like minor details just before a race can often be the difference between mediocre and peak performance.

This chapter includes physiologically based information that will allow you to optimize your performance on race day. The right racing tactics will help you run your best time possible or beat an important rival. Warming up properly will ensure that you're ready to race at your best when the starting gun fires, and cooling down correctly will aid your recovery from racing. Glycogen (carbohydrate) loading will help you maintain race pace during long races. Tapering, or reducing your mileage and intensity before an important race, enables you to reach your potential. And sound recovery in the weeks following a marathon will help you ease the transition to your next racing goal. Managing these details well will allow you to get the most from the hard training you've done before your goal race.

Racing Tactics

The two adversaries in distance running are your competitors and the clock. Your racing tactics depend on which of these adversaries is more important in a specific race. To beat other runners of equal ability, you need to run smarter than they do. To beat the clock, you simply need to run the fastest time possible, which runners usually accomplish with even pacing. So, first decide on your objective for a given race and then select the tactics to meet that objective. Finally, during training, visualize yourself successfully using those tactics to achieve your objective.

Running an even pace is the most effective way to run the fastest time because it uses oxygen most economically and keeps lactate accumulation to a minimum. Most distance world records are set by running an even pace. Consider the 10,000-meter world record of 26:22.75 that Haile Gebre Silasie set on June 1, 1998: His two 5,000-meter halves took 13:11.7 and 13:11.0; except for a fast closing kilometer, his kilometer splits varied by no more than 5 seconds (from 2:35.8 to 2:40.8). Any way you parse it, Gebre Silasie's run was a model of economical racing.

Even pacing requires that you know the correct pace to select, that you have good pace judgment, and that you have the discipline to hold back in the early stages of the race, when the pace feels easy. The best time to learn race pace is during training. When you learn what it feels like to run at your goal pace, it becomes natural for you to maintain that pace during the race. The race-training schedules later in this book include training at your goal-race pace.

Running even splits is also often a good way to beat other runners. By running an even pace, you'll gradually catch runners who started too fast. Catching and passing other runners during the race will give you a psychological lift and will weigh heavily on the other runners.

The best racing strategy depends on the conditions, the course, and your goals.

Of course, you don't know whether the other runners will come back to you; you may let someone go in a race and never catch her. If you run evenly, however, you'll have the best chance of beating someone who has started too fast. Running an even pace is also your best tactic for beating someone who starts off slowly and tries to pick up the pace during the race. If you run evenly, the other runner won't get the psychological reinforcement of making up ground on you quickly. The other runner will also be using energy less economically, so if she does catch you, you'll be able to hold her off.

In some situations, you may find it necessary to abandon the even-pacing rule and start the race somewhat faster than the pace you can maintain for the entire distance. For example, suppose it's important to you to beat a specific runner. If your rival starts quickly, you may want to run a bit more aggressively so the other runner doesn't build too big a lead. Chances are that the other runner will pay a high price for the fast early pace, and you'll catch her later in the race. These are often the tactics you'll use in cross-country races.

Environmental conditions can also affect your racing tactics. On a windy day, you're best off running with other people. To stay in a group of runners you may have to run slightly faster or slower than you otherwise would. Try to let the others do most of the work blocking the wind for you. If the pace is slowing, you may want to suggest to the other runners that you take turns leading into the wind. (Of course, the other runners may tell you where to go.) This will help the group overall, and may help you all catch and pass other runners. Similarly, on a hot day, you need to reconsider your pace. Jack Fultz won the 1976 Boston Marathon in 90-degree heat by wisely choosing a conservative pace early in the race, then steadily passing other runners as they wilted in the heat.

If you're catching someone in a road race and want to pass him, do so gradually, and run just behind him until you're ready to make a decisive move. Then run by strongly and keep your momentum until you've built at least a 30-yard lead. At this point, he'll lose contact with you mentally. Never look back to see where someone is. This gives the runners behind you a psychological boost by letting them know that you're tired and worried about them. (You may very well be, but they don't have to know it.)

Changing Plans

Successful racing also requires flexibility. Always have a plan going into the race but be willing to alter your plan if conditions require it. At the 1984 Olympic Marathon Trials, my prerace plan was to stay in the second pack and gradually pass people during the race. When the leaders slowed at halfway, however, I picked up the pace. When no one went with me, I had to decide whether to ease off and be absorbed back into the pack or to forge ahead and try to build my lead. I decided to keep pushing the pace and hope that I could hold on and make the Olympic team. As it turned out, I built a 30-second lead on the pack, which included Alberto Salazar, Greg Meyer, and Bill Rodgers. At 25 miles, Salazar and John Tuttle passed me. By hanging on to them for dear life, I made the team and outsprinted Alberto at the finish to win the race. The change of racing plans proved to be a good decision.—Peter Pfitzinger

© Victah

Co-author Pete Pfitzinger won the 1984 Olympic Marathon Trials by having a flexible race plan.

Warming Up and Cooling Down

An important part of the physiological preparation for any race is the warm-up. Unfortunately, many runners go about their warm-ups rather casually. After months of serious training, it's a shame to turn in a less-than-optimal performance by failing to warm up properly. On the flip side, your recovery from racing or an intense workout begins with the cool-down, a simple, effective way to ensure that your training continues to progress.

Warming Up

The shorter the race, the more vital the warm-up. That's because in shorter races you need to be able to launch into $\dot{V}O_2$max pace or faster right from the start. Doing so when you're not properly warmed up causes a large amount of lactate to form in your muscles early in the race. When this happens, you fatigue quickly and your finishing time suffers.

The physiological purpose of the warm-up is to increase your metabolic rate (heart rate, oxygen consumption, etc.) to the level they must reach during the initial stages of the race. Because your metabolism works at a low level when you're at rest, your body can't shift instantly into high gear. The warm-up bridges the gap between resting and racing by initiating hormonal changes, increasing core temperature and muscle temperature, shifting blood distribution, and causing metabolic changes. With your metabolism working at a higher level, your cardiovascular system is ready to transport oxygen to your muscles and your muscles are ready to produce energy aerobically when the race starts.

Start warming up about 45 minutes before the start of the race. Run one to two miles, beginning slowly and gradually increasing the pace so that you run the last quarter to half mile at your lactate-threshold pace. Now your cardiovascular system is working at a higher level, and your metabolic rate has increased substantially. Next, stretch gently for 15 minutes or so, focusing your attention on your strategy for the race. Approximately 15 minutes before the start of the race, run an easy mile, then do several accelerations of 100 to 200 meters up to race pace. Plan your warm-up so that you complete it no more than 5 minutes before the start of the race. If you finish your warm-up too soon, your heart rate and metabolic rate will decrease, and you will lose some of the benefits of the warm-up. If you're in a large race where the organizers assemble the field well before the start, keep moving, even if it means running in place, so that your heart rate remains elevated.

Warming up for a marathon is different. In the marathon, glycogen depletion is a limiting factor in performance; it doesn't make sense to expend much of your precious fuel stores on warming up. You just need to be ready to run at your goal pace, so run half a mile or so, gradually working down to your goal-race pace. Also, don't do the fast accelerations that you would do before shorter races. Because you run accelerations at high intensity, they burn primarily glycogen, which you'll need late in the marathon.

Cooling Down

The purpose of the cool-down is to help return your body to preexercise conditions. This includes reducing your heart rate, your breathing rate, your core body temperature, and the levels of hormones such as epinephrine (adrenaline) in your blood. After races of 10K or shorter, an important role of the cool-down is to remove the lactate that has accumulated in your muscles and blood. By running slowly for a cool-down, you keep your circulation going, which helps to clear the lactate from your muscles and blood more quickly. Your cool-down should consist of easy running for one to three miles. If you're too tired to run, brisk walking is the best alternative.

As with warming up, the marathon is the exception here. Even the best runners in the world don't do cool-down jogs after a marathon. Still, you should try to keep moving after you finish, so that your muscles don't tighten more than they already have. For more on what to do after a marathon, see the section on marathon recovery later in this chapter.

Glycogen Loading

The two factors that conspire to make you slow in the last few miles of the marathon—or any event that takes longer than an hour and a half to complete—are glycogen depletion and dehydration. We discussed the dangers of dehydration in chapter 4. Now, let's see what you can do to combat glycogen depletion.

First, let's review the background physiology. The two primary fuels used for endurance exercise are carbohydrate and fat. Carbohydrate is stored in the body as glycogen. Fat is stored in the body as, well, you know. When you run, your body burns a mixture of carbohydrate and fat. The harder you run, the more carbohydrate

Marathons require proper pacing to best use your body's fuel stores.

you use; the slower you run, the more fat you use. Because you're reading this book, it's probably a safe assumption that you want to complete the marathon as quickly as you can. Marathoners who race the distance most likely burn 80 to 90 percent carbohydrate (glycogen) and 10 to 20 percent fat during the race.

As your glycogen stores become progressively depleted during the run, your body tries to conserve what's left by burning more fat. The breakdown of fat requires more oxygen per calorie released than does carbohydrate, meaning that fat is a less efficient energy source; when you have to burn more fat, you slow. A problem with glycogen depletion is that warning signs don't appear until it's too late. When you suddenly have to slow late in a marathon, it's probably glycogen depletion that got you, rather than dehydration, which tends to affect you more slowly.

As we discussed in chapter 3, pure endurance training helps your long-race performance by delaying the point at which glycogen depletion becomes a problem. Training achieves this through two adaptations. First, as you become more endurance trained, your muscles restock their glycogen stores at a higher level than do untrained muscles. Second, your muscles become trained to conserve glycogen by using more fat at a given pace.

Unfortunately, the marathon is so long that even well-trained runners will deplete their glycogen stores during the race if they don't have a sound plan for taking in extra carbohydrate before and during the event. If you eat a normal runner's diet, with about 60 percent of your calories from carbohydrate, you probably store 1,500 to 2,000 calories of glycogen in your muscles. If you glycogen load, however, your muscles have the capacity to store 2,300 to 2,700 calories of glycogen. Each mile that you run burns 90 to 140 calories, depending on your weight and metabolism. If you do a great job of loading, you'll have just about enough glycogen for a marathon. If you don't load, your glycogen stores will be only partially filled. As a result, you could start to run low on glycogen any time after 90 minutes of running and end up struggling to the finish line wondering what happened.

Glycogen loading is also important before any training run lasting more than 90 minutes. The last thing you want, both physically and psychologically, is to struggle home in your long runs. If you focus on carbohydrates and hydration for the day or two before your long runs, you'll increase your chances for a better training effort and a positive psychological experience.

What is glycogen loading? Popularly known as carboloading, the practice has been popular since the late 1960s, when Per-Olof Åstrand showed that athletes can almost double their muscle glycogen stores by running a long run seven days before a race, eating a low-carbohydrate diet for three days, and then eating a high-carbohydrate diet (70 to 80 percent of calories from carbohydrates) for the three days preceding the race. The long run depletes your body's glycogen stores; the three days of low carbohydrate intake keeps them low. This triggers a mechanism in your body to store as much carbohydrate as possible. The downside is that by day three of the low-carbohydrate diet, you'll probably feel weak and irritable, and your loved ones will avoid you.

Fortunately, more recent research has shown that you can elevate glycogen stores to similar levels without the long run and low carbohydrate phases. Here's how: Eat your normal diet until three days before the race while reducing your mileage by half. During those last three days, eat a high-carbohydrate diet (70 to 80 percent of calories from carbohydrates) and run just a few easy miles each day. Your body will store glycogen at a level similar to what it would using Åstrand's program.

Good sources of carbohydrates are rice, pasta, bread, sweet potatoes, pancakes, bagels, potatoes, and corn. Be sure that you're consuming extra carbohydrate, not extra fat. Fettuccine Alfredo, for example, contains plenty of carbohydrate but also a lot of fat because of the heavy cream sauce. Many of the world's best marathoners eat rice for their prerace meal because it provides plenty of carbohydrates and is easy to digest. You should expect to gain a couple of pounds when you glycogen load because your body stores 2.6 grams of water for every gram of glycogen. Don't be alarmed by the added weight. It's inevitable, and the stored water will help prevent dehydration during the race.

Carbing on the Run

Carbohydrate loading before the event is a sufficient precaution against glycogen depletion for races up to about two hours long. For the marathon, however, you're still at risk. The solution is to take in additional calories during the race.

The easiest way to consume carbohydrate on the run is in a sport drink or energy gel. Sport drinks have the added benefit of providing needed fluid at the same time. Research has shown that the stronger the concentration of sugars and electrolytes in a drink, the longer it takes to empty from your stomach. Because there's little risk of seriously depleting your electrolyte stores in races up to the marathon, you don't need to replace electrolytes until after the race.

The trick is to find a balance between a carbohydrate solution that's strong enough to give you needed calories but not so strong that it's absorbed slowly from your stomach. Solutions containing 4 to 8 percent carbohydrates are generally optimal. Most runners' stomachs can absorb only about 7 ounces of liquid every 15 minutes. Drinking 28 ounces per hour of a 4 percent solution will supply 32 grams of carbohydrate, while an 8 percent solution will supply 64 grams of carbohydrate. Each gram of carbohydrate contains 4.1 calories, so with this plan you'll take in 130 to 260 calories per hour. If you run the marathon in three hours, then you'd take in 400 to 800 calories during the race. That's enough carbohydrate fuel to last an extra five to ten miles. Energy gels have recently become popular because of their convenience. You can carry them from the start and take them when you want, and they're an easy way to take in at least a few hundred more calories. Most contain about 100 calories in an easily digested, pudding-like substance that comes in a packet that fits in the palm of your hand. It's important to plan when to take energy gels during the race—they're most effective when followed by several swallows of liquid, so try to finish them just before you reach an aid station or will otherwise be getting fluid.

Try your carbohydrate of choice during your training runs. Practice swallowing energy gels at marathon pace. Find out which sport drink will be supplied at your marathon and try it during training.

Table 5.1 Sport Drinks and Gels

Drinks	Calories per 8 oz. serving	Carbohydrates	Potassium
All-Sport	70	17 g	7%
Gatorade	55	13 g	6%
Powerade	70	17 g	7%
Exceed	70	50 g	7%
XLR8	168	42 g	7%

Gels	Calories per container	Carbohydrates
Vanilla Bean Gu	100	25 g
Chocolate Hammer Gel	100	20 g
Lemon Lime Pocket Rocket	100	25 g
Vanilla PowerGel	110	28 g
Lemon Lime Squeezy	80	20 g
Ultra Gel	133	24 g

Rehearse grabbing cups and swallowing liquid on the run without choking. When you know which drinks and gels work for you, develop a plan for consuming carbohydrate during the race, such as having friends positioned along the course to give you supplies.

Tapering

"Train hard to race well" is the runner's mantra. Everything we do is based on hard work: We brave the elements, we endure, we run through blizzards and bronchitis, we don't wimp out. And we certainly don't rest. This puritanical philosophy impels us to drag our bodies out on the roads day after day after day. With hard work and consistency, we grow stronger and faster.

A time comes, however, when working harder is counterproductive to performance. That time is the last three weeks before a marathon and the several days before shorter races. That's the time to taper—to reduce significantly the volume and intensity of your training. Let's start by looking at the distance that most requires a good taper, the marathon.

Most runners take it increasingly easier during the last 10 days or so before a marathon. That's good, but not enough, or more accurately, too much. How do you know if you don't usually taper enough? Have you ever hit the wall in the last few miles of a marathon despite doing all the right training? If so, you've probably worked too hard in the days before the race. A well-executed taper will give you extra reserves—reserves that will push the wall out past the finish line and perhaps make the difference between whether you maintain your pace or struggle home over the last six miles.

Despite the benefits, tapering is the most overlooked phase of marathon preparation. But tapering is no less necessary than long runs are to reaching peak strength on race day. Tapering allows your muscles to repair the microdamage of intervals and long runs, permits your muscles and liver to store glycogen, helps your body to overcome the constant dehydration of hard training, and relieves that last bit of tendinitis in your knee or ankle or hip.

Again, to taper effectively for a marathon takes about three weeks. Unfortunately, our self-confidence is fragile. Our egos require the positive reinforcement of a hard workout every few days. If we take a few days easy—let alone three weeks—we go through withdrawal. Our distance-runners' paranoia makes us fear that our muscles will turn to mush and that we'll waste all those months of hard work.

By tapering properly, co-author Pete Pfitzinger was able to get the most from his training.

Despair not. Studies have shown that runners can cut back on their training by 60 percent for three weeks with no decrease in running performance or $\dot{V}O_2$max. A well-planned marathon taper cuts the volume of your running while keeping you working hard enough to stay in peak condition and get your training fix. The marathon schedules in chapter 9 give day-by-day workouts for the three weeks before the marathon, using these guidelines: First, allow two recovery days for each hard effort. Second, both your hard days and easy days should decrease in volume as you get closer to the race. To see these principles put into practice, see the schedules in chapter 9.

Tapering for Shorter Races

Prerace tapering is also important for distances shorter than a marathon. A study at the Human Performance Laboratory at East Carolina University supports the benefits of tapering for shorter races. The study comprised three well-matched groups of runners—a run-taper group, a cycle-taper group, and a control group. During a seven-day period, the run-taper group ran 400-meter intervals at 5K race pace and cut their training volume by 85 percent. The cycle-taper group performed roughly the same training as the run-taper group but trained exclusively on a cycle ergometer. The control group continued with their normal training of approximately six miles per day and two or three days per week of interval training or fartlek.

The study found that those in the run-taper group improved their performance in a 5K time trial by about 2.8 percent, roughly 30 seconds for these runners. Runners in the cycle-taper and control groups didn't improve significantly. The study suggests that drastic reductions in training volume combined with intervals can significantly improve race performance.

Research on tapering, however, is still in its infancy, and this study's particular run-taper approach may not be the most beneficial combination of speed and volume. Until more research is conducted, a more conservative approach, such as cutting back your training by 50 percent, should provide most of the benefit of a more severe taper. A good rule of thumb is to taper one day for each two kilometers of the race. For example, you would taper for about 5 days before a 10K or 10 days before a half marathon (21K). The schedules in chapters 6, 7, 8, and 10 incorporate these principles as you approach your goal race.

Marathon Recovery

You follow the schedules, taper perfectly, and run the marathon of your life. You wake up the next morning stiff and sore. Now what?

For the next couple days, try walking downstairs backward. Why? That's where the kitchen and the rest of the world are, and your quadriceps scream at you if go downstairs the conventional way. But they've earned the right to scream—you've just pounded them on the hard pavement more than 25,000 times.

How long will it take to recover? Although the scientific literature hasn't provided clear-cut guidelines, the common rule of thumb is to take one recovery day for each mile of the race. That sounds simple. Twenty-six recovery days after a marathon sounds pretty darned good. But what's a recovery day? Does it mean you sit around with your feet up? Does it mean easy running is OK, but no intervals? Here's how to recover quickly while reducing the likelihood of postmarathon breakdown.

First Few Hours

Stay warm. Avoid finishing the marathon and standing around getting progressively colder. This will cause your muscles to get even

What you do soon after a marathon contributes to how quickly you recover.

stiffer than they already are (if that's possible). Also, your immune system is depressed after a marathon, so you're at a greater risk of infection. Arrange to have warm clothes at the finish area. Walk around after putting them on. Your feet will likely be swollen and blistered, so also bring a roomy pair of shoes or sandals to change into.

Drink. After any marathon, you'll be dehydrated. The warmer the day, the more dehydrated you'll be. So drink plenty of fluids after the race. Your thirst mechanism is imperfect—when you're no longer thirsty, your body may still need fluid. Drink until you have to urinate and until your urine is clear in color.

Eat. When you run a marathon, you deplete your glycogen stores. Recent studies have shown that your muscles will replace their glycogen stores at the fastest rate during the first 1 to 2 hours after running. Glycogen resynthesis continues at a higher than normal rate for 10 to 12 hours after a glycogen-depleting run. This means that you'll recover more quickly if you take in carbohydrate soon after you finish the race. If your stomach doesn't feel up to a meal, eat a bagel or a banana, or drink some carbohydrate to start the replenishment process. Eat more when your stomach can handle it. Continue to eat carbohydrate-rich foods for at least two days after a marathon because your muscles need time to reload fully.

First Few Days

During the first three to seven days after the marathon, you'll learn all about DOMS, or delayed-onset muscle soreness. This condition is caused by microscopic damage to muscle fibers and the surrounding connective tissue as a result of eccentric muscle contractions, which are lengthening or braking contractions. When you run downhill, your quadriceps contract eccentrically to keep your knees from buckling when your feet strike the ground. If you've just run the Boston Marathon, you know all about this. Likewise, when you run down the bridge into Manhattan 16 miles into the New York City Marathon, your quads contract eccentrically like mad. That's why you're walking downstairs backwards. Because it takes a while for the process of damage, inflammation, and pain to occur, DOMS is generally most severe 24 to 72 hours after exercise.

So this DOMS thing sounds painful. What should you do for the first few days after the marathon? Get a massage. Go swimming. Ride a bike. Take a walk. But don't run until the soreness in your muscles subsides. Their resiliency is at an all-time low, and your risk of injury is high. These other forms of gentle exercise, however, will pump blood to your muscles and help you recover more quickly.

There's another reason to skip running for a few days after the race. Eventually, your warped judgment will lead you to start training for another race. You will be getting up at 5:30, running in the dark through snow, rain, and hail. Your mind needs a break, too. During this recess, indulge yourself. Eat kahlua mocha fudge brownie ice cream. Sleep in. Get thrown out of the local hot tub. In short, give your brain a rest from the discipline of training.

First Few Weeks

After the first week, the soreness in your muscles should be gone. If your muscles still feel stiff and you can afford it, a massage during the second week of marathon recovery can work wonders.

You're probably compulsive enough to consider resuming training after a week or so. How should you rebuild your mileage? Try a premarathon taper in reverse. After a few days off from running, jog a couple of miles per day on a soft surface to finish off the first postmarathon week. Then run 50 percent of your usual weekly mileage the second week and 75 percent the third week. To ensure a complete recovery, run at moderate intensity, keeping your heart rate below 70 percent of your heart-rate reserve or 80 percent of your maximal heart rate.

At the end of the third week, try running half a mile at your 10K race pace. If you're able to run fluidly, with no residual stiffness, you're ready to graduate to your normal training routine. If, however, you're still a bit stiff in the calves or quads or hamstrings, give yourself another week at 75 percent of your normal mileage with no speedwork. Then try the test again. After you've passed this recovery test, you're ready to resume speedwork. Start with a relatively gentle session, running about two-thirds of your usual volume of intervals.

After three to four weeks of normal training (six to eight weeks postmarathon), you should be completely recovered from the marathon and ready to consider racing. Be warned: The first race after a marathon is usually a blow to the ego because all the training for the marathon has made you strong but slow and you haven't yet had time to rebuild your speed. Consider the first race a benchmark against which to measure future improvement.

Now that we've looked at the hows and whys of preparing for top distance running, let's apply those principles. In the rest of the book, we'll show you the best way to prepare for the most popular races, starting with the 5K.

PART II

TRAINING FOR PEAK PERFORMANCE

CHAPTER 6

Training to Race 5K

© Victah

This chapter focuses on the 5K (5,000 meters), the shortest race covered in this book yet the least forgiving. That's because during a 5K race, you run almost at your $\dot{V}O_2$max. The consequence of this physiological fact is that if you go out too hard, your muscles don't receive oxygen quickly enough and lactate rapidly builds up in your muscles, forcing you to slow. Finding your optimal pace is crucial to success in this event.

Physiology of the 5K

Whether the sport is running, cycling, cross-country skiing, rowing, or swimming, $\dot{V}O_2$max is the most important physiological variable determining success in events lasting between 3 minutes and 20 minutes. In running, this includes races of 1,500 meters to 5,000 meters. Because you run the 5K above your lactate threshold, your lactate levels increase continuously during the race. If you plan your effort optimally, your lactate level will become distressingly high just as you are reaching the finish line.

Because a high $\dot{V}O_2$max is most important to success at this distance, the 5K is physiologically unique among the races covered in this book; in the others, a high lactate threshold is at least as important as $\dot{V}O_2$max. The 5K is also distinct from the longer races because a significant portion of the energy you use in a 5K is supplied anaerobically. For example, although less than 1 percent of the energy for a marathon is supplied anaerobically, 5 to 10 percent of energy production is anaerobic when you race a 5K.

Selecting Your Goal Pace

If you've raced a 5K before, you know roughly what your finishing time will be. Set realistic goals for your next race. If you set your best time last year and are preparing for your first race of the season, shoot for a solid performance rather than a personal best. After you have a couple of races under your belt, then you should be ready to go after personal bests.

If you've never raced a 5K, or if you've run 5Ks but haven't focused on them, you can estimate your 5K time by converting your times from other distances. Table 6.1 shows the conversion factors from 8K (which is 7 to 12 seconds shorter than 5 miles), 10K, 15K, 10 miles, 20K, and half marathons to the 5K. The table doesn't provide a conversion from the marathon to the 5K because the margin of error

Table 6.1   Conversion Factors to Estimate 5K Time

8K-5 miles	10K	15K	10 miles	20K	Half marathon
.602	.478	.309	.284	.226	.213

is too great, depending on whether you're more of a mid-distance runner who dabbles in the marathon or a dyed-in-the-wool marathoner.

To predict your 5K time from your 8K, 10K, 15K, 10-mile, 20K, or half-marathon times, multiply the total number of seconds from your finishing times for those races by .602, .478, .309, .284, .226, or .213, respectively. For example, if your 10K time is 40:00 (2,400 seconds), your predicted 5K time would be 1,147 seconds (2,400 × .478), which equals 19:07. For a table of equivalencies among distances, see the appendix.

Training for the 5K

This chapter includes schedules for runners who typically train (a) less than 20 miles per week, (b) 20 to 40 miles per week, and (c) more than 40 miles per week. Regardless of your training mileage, the schedules are based on the physiological demands of the race. Your racing objective is to run as fast as you can for 5K. Your training objective is to increase your $\dot{V}O_2$max and prepare physically and mentally to run as close as possible to your $\dot{V}O_2$max for the duration of the race.

In preparing to race 5K, you cannot ignore any of the four types of training discussed in chapters 2 and 3. The 5K schedules were developed according to the priorities shown in table 6.2. Before the start of the schedule, when months remain until your goal race, your training should concentrate on building endurance. Your highest priorities should be pure endurance training and lactate-threshold training. These will give you the base upon which to build your $\dot{V}O_2$max and 5K performance. The base training schedules in chapter 4 will prepare you to start the schedules in this chapter.

During the first 6 weeks of the schedule, you'll continue to work on endurance. The schedules gradually increase the distance of the long run and the second long run, as well as the total weekly mileage.

Libbie Hickman

© Victah

5K Personal Record: 15:11
Career highlight at distance: 7th, 1997 World Championships
   Training and racing emphasis: Libbie Hickman has extended her range in recent years after initially making her reputation as a 3K/5K runner on the track, who would usually not venture beyond 10Ks on the road. As she's increased her mileage and raced with success at more distances, she's become more of a force at shorter track races. In 1997, she won the Bolder Boulder 10K in late May. A few weeks later, she won the US outdoor championships at 5,000m, then ran a personal record in the heat of Athens to take seventh at that distance at the World Championships.
   For the first few months of the year, Hickman builds strength with 90+ miles per week. She doesn't race much, if at all, during this base-building phase. Even as track season nears, she competes infrequently, owing to the lack of top-class opportunities near her home in Ft. Collins, CO. Hickman compensates for this lack of tune-ups with what she calls "race-simulation workouts," in which she runs three miles of intervals with short rests. For example, Hickman will do a workout of 12 × 300m at 5K race pace with 100m recovery; rather than jogging the rest, however, she recovers at a good clip, so that she averages close to 5:10 per mile for the 12 laps. Starting in late April, Hickman starts to run workouts at a goal pace of :72 per lap, which is just slightly faster than her 5K personal record pace. "The idea is to make 5,000m pace comfortable," she says. During the summer, she sometimes drops her mileage to less than 50 miles per week, roughly half of her peak mileage, to stay fresh and focused on the demands of peak speed training and racing. After track season, Hickman moves to longer road races in the fall.
   An important facet of Hickman's training year-round is that she does a lot of striders. "It's important not to neglect your speed," she says. "I do them [striders] a couple of times a week after easy runs." Some of Hickman's strider sessions are on grass and include a slight downhill section to maximize her speed development.

6.2	**Priorities for 5K Training, in Order of Importance During the Schedule**		
	Preschedule	**First 6 weeks**	**Last 6 weeks**
Basic speed	4	4	3
$\dot{V}O_2$max	3	1	1
Lactate threshold	2	2	2
Pure endurance	1	3	4

$\dot{V}O_2$max training, however, is the top training priority throughout the 12 weeks. During the last 6 weeks of the schedule, you maintain endurance and emphasize $\dot{V}O_2$max and final preparations for your goal race.

Schedules Explained

The training schedules are 12 weeks long, which is enough time to provide a powerful training stimulus to improve performance but not so long that you lose focus on the event. The schedules are organized vertically by the number of weeks until the race, so that your goal race is always your reference point. By looking down any one of the columns, you can easily see how the workouts progress during the 12 weeks for that type of training.

The schedules are also organized horizontally, so that you can quickly view the key workouts for the week. In this way, it's easy to get a feel for the types of training stimuli being emphasized that week, as well as to see that you won't be doing too much in any week. What the schedules don't do is recommend which days of the week to do which workout; that depends on the schedule that organizes the rest of your life.

Longest run   This is simply the longest run for the week. The schedules gradually increase your long run during the first six weeks to help prepare you for the endurance component of the race. For runners training more than 40 miles per week, the long run starts at 8 miles and increases to 11 miles. For runners training less than 20 miles per week, the long runs start at 5 miles and increase to 7 miles. Remember, long runs aren't jogs—to stimulate desirable physiological adaptations, such as increased capillary

Bob Kennedy

© Victah

5K Personal Record: 12:58
Career highlights at distance: American records at 3,000m, 2 miles, and 5,000m
Training and racing emphasis: Bob Kennedy's focus is the summer European track circuit. Every year he bases his running on producing top efforts against the best of the rest of the world at the 3,000m and 5,000m. He runs at other distances and venues during the year—in December 1997, for example, he placed second at the US national cross-country championships at a distance of 12K—but other races are always used as part of his preparation for summer track racing. Kennedy avoids road races, saying that even to dabble in them would detract from his ability to reach his goals on the track. His focus obviously works as since 1994 he has been a significant player in nearly every important world-class 5,000m on the track. In 1996, he became the first non-African to break 13:00 for the distance.

Says Kennedy about being a 5K specialist, "At any time during the year, there has to be an element of base, $\dot{V}O_2$max workouts, and speedwork in your training. Depending on the time of year, you'll be focusing on one of these elements. In the spring—late March, April, May, and early June—my primary focus is on strength—that is, working at my $\dot{V}O_2$max pace. The key training is done at distances of 800m to 2,000m at goal-race pace. I think it's important to emphasize goal-race pace. Too many athletes train at current race pace, which is something they've already achieved."

Kennedy's American record at 3,000m involves a pace of 4:01 per 1,600m, or just more than 60 seconds per lap. His 5,000m record is a pace of 4:08 per 1,600m, or :62 per lap. Here are two examples of the $\dot{V}O_2$max workouts Kennedy does during this period.

Workout #1: 2,000m in 5:10; 3:00 rest; 1,600m in 4:06; 3:00 rest; 1,200m in 3:03; 3:00 rest; 800m in 2:00; 3:00 rest; 400m in :58.

Workout #2: 4 × 1,600m in 4:04 to 4:08 with 3:00 rest after each.

Says Kennedy, "These are just a couple of examples and shouldn't be portrayed as the only workouts that accomplish this particular goal." About maintaining balance in training while emphasizing $\dot{V}O_2$ max workouts, he says, "Remember that you still need to incorporate base and speed into your training, even though at this time of year you're focusing on strength. Do your long runs and a couple of workouts that turn your legs over."

density, do your long runs 1:30 to 2:30 per mile slower than your 5K race pace.

Second longest run   This is the second longest run for the week. The purpose of these sessions is to reinforce the training adaptations of the long runs. These runs increase in distance in a similar pattern to the long runs.

Lactate-threshold workouts   The workouts in this column include tempo runs, LT intervals, time trials, and tune-up races. We explained tempo runs and LT intervals in detail in chapter 3. Tempo runs are continuous runs of 20 to 40 minutes at lactate-threshold pace. Lactate-threshold pace is approximately your 15K to half-marathon race pace. (For other ways to estimate lactate-threshold pace, see chapter 3.) For these workouts, warm up for about two miles, run the tempo run at lactate-threshold pace, and then cool down for a mile or two. Run LT intervals at the same pace as tempo runs but instead of one continuous run, break the distance into two to four segments, with several minutes of slow running following each one.

Time trials and tune-up races are more intense than tempo runs or LT intervals. Time trials involve running as fast as you can in training for a given distance. They give you a good indication of how ready you are to race. Tune-up races are competitions that you enter as part of your buildup. The schedules include tune-up races that are both longer and shorter than 5K. Time trials and tune-up races serve the additional purpose of preparing you mentally for peak performance. During the 12 weeks, the lactate-threshold workouts progress from LT intervals and tempo runs to time trials and tune-up races. This schedule builds to a close simulation of the demands of your goal race.

$\dot{V}O_2$max workouts   These workouts are intervals of 600 meters to 2,000 meters. You can run these workouts on a track, a golf course, grass fields, trails, or uphill. As discussed in chapter 2, the most effective way to improve $\dot{V}O_2$max is to train at an intensity that requires 95 to 100 percent of your current $\dot{V}O_2$max. This approximates your 3K to 5K race pace. The schedules gradually increase the pace of these workouts to 5K goal pace as your fitness improves. To recover between intervals, you should run slowly for a time that lasts 50 to 90 percent of the interval's duration.

Basic speed   The goal of these workouts is to improve your leg turnover and running form. By doing so you will increase your finishing speed, which is important for success in the 5K. Basic speed sessions involve short repetitions of 100 to 200 meters. We include these workouts because of the importance of anaerobic energy production to 5K racing.

Putting it all together   As an example of how to structure the week's training, look at nine weeks to go on Schedule B (20 to 40 miles per week). The schedule for that week includes four workouts. Do easy recovery runs or cross-training as necessary to reach the total of 30 miles for the week (table 6.3). For how to equate cross-training with running mileage, see chapter 4.

A typical way to complete that week's training is to do the longest run on Sunday, followed by a day off on Monday. Tuesday could be a recovery day consisting of an easy 4 miles. Wednesday would be time for a hard session, such as the $\dot{V}O_2$max workout. Thursday could

Table 6.3	Properly Structuring a Sample Week From 5K Schedule B
Sunday	8 miles
Monday	Off
Tuesday	4 miles
Wednesday	$\dot{V}O_2$max workout (7 miles, including warm-up, 4 × 1K intervals, and cool-down)
Thursday	6 miles
Friday	Off
Saturday	5 miles, including striders
Mileage for week	30

be the second longest run, followed by a day off on Friday. The week could end with 10 × 100 meters as part of a 5-mile run on Saturday. You complete the 30 miles in five days of running, with the workouts spaced evenly throughout the week.

Avoid doing important workouts on consecutive days. If your personal schedule requires that you do most of your hard running on the weekends, try to follow the two hard days with two easy days for recovery.

If you miss an important workout, don't try to make it up. For example, if injury, fatigue, bad weather, or demands from the rest of your life put you behind schedule early in the week, don't run several hard sessions in a row to make up for lost time. If you try to squeeze several hard sessions together, the quality of your workouts will go down and you'll increase your risk of injury. Instead, use the priorities outlined in table 6.2 to determine the most important sessions for where you are in the schedule. For example, say you're following Schedule B and with five weeks to go before your goal race, you can fit in only two important workouts. According to table 6.2, your top training priorities among the workouts scheduled for the week during this period are developing your $\dot{V}O_2$max and basic speed. Therefore, you would do the 7 × 600-meter session listed as the week's $\dot{V}O_2$max workout on one day, and the 10 × 100-meter session listed as the week's basic speed workout on another day.

Runners following Schedule C who want to do more than the weekly mileage listed in the schedule should follow the trend in mileage and simply adjust their mileage upward as a percentage of the prescribed mileage. For example, say that you want to reach a peak mileage of 75 per week; this would occur with five weeks to go. As noted in Schedule C, with one week to go, you should reach roughly 70 percent of your peak, or 52 miles (75 × 70 percent). Follow this principle throughout the program to ensure that your mileage builds in the first part of the schedule, then tapers as you approach your goal race.

Racing Strategy and Mental Approach

Whether you're racing 5K on the roads or on the track, the race is challenging, both physically and mentally. Physically, the 5K is tough because you're racing at just about your $\dot{V}O_2$max, so you have little margin for error in selecting your race pace. If you start too slowly, you can't make up the time lost later in the race. Worse, and more

© Victah

Christine Pfitzinger has mastered the art of pacing in a 5K.

typical, if you go out too fast, your muscles will accumulate lactate too quickly. You'll have to slow, and your finishing time won't be all that suffers. The secret to a great 5K, therefore, is selecting the fastest pace that you can maintain for the distance. Your $\dot{V}O_2$max workouts will give you a good idea of how fast that pace will be.

Mentally, the 5K is tough because you must concentrate for the entire race. In longer races, you can let your mind wander a bit during the middle miles. During a 5K, however, the effort you need to maintain is so intense that you cannot allow a lapse in concentration. Fortunately, you can learn to maintain your focus during training. Rehearse running fast yet relaxed and become aware of how to find the fastest pace that you can hold without tightening up.

One way to help you achieve your best result in a 5K is to warm up thoroughly for the start of the race. Although important for all races, a good warm-up is vital in the 5K because you don't have the luxury of getting up to speed slowly—as soon as the gun fires, you need to be able to launch into your $\dot{V}O_2$max pace. A thorough warm-up should begin about 45 minutes before the start of the race. Include 1+ to 3 miles of easy running, stretching, and several accelerations of 100 to 200 meters up to race pace.

At the end of a 5K, you can kick with reckless abandon; you get to stop soon, so it doesn't matter if you accumulate high levels of lactate. To beat your rival in a 5K, the best strategy is to run an even pace. If you're with him in the last half mile, run off his shoulder until you're confident that you can make a sustained sprint to the finish. This will usually be with 100 to 200 meters to go. Avoid the temptation to start your sprint too early or you may find your rival running off your shoulder with one gear left.

5K Training Schedule
Schedule A: Less than 20 miles/week

Weeks to goal	LR1	LR2	Lactate-threshold workouts	$\dot{V}O_2$max workouts	Basic speed workouts	Week's mileage
11	5	4	–	5 × 600 meters at current 5K pace	–	14
10	6	4	2 × 1 1/2-mile LT intervals	–	–	15
9	5	4	–	4 × 800 meters at 2–3 sec/lap slower than 5K goal pace	–	16
8	6	4	3-mile tempo run	–	10 × 100 meters	17
7	6	5	–	3 × 1K at 1–2 sec/lap slower than 5K goal pace	–	17
6	6	5	3K or 2-mile time trial	–	10 × 100 meters	18
5	7	6	–	6 × 600 meters at 5K goal pace	–	20
4	7	5	3-mile tempo run	–	10 × 100 meters	20
3	7	5	–	4 × 1K at 5K goal pace	–	20
2	6	5	3K or 2-mile race	–	10 × 100 meters	18
1	6	4	–	2 × 1,600 meters at 5K goal pace	–	16
Race week	5	3	**Goal 5K race**	–	10 × 100 meters	14

5K Training Schedule
Schedule B: 20–40 miles/week

Weeks to goal	LR1	LR2	Lactate-threshold workouts	V̇O₂max workouts	Basic speed workouts	Week's mileage
11	6	5	–	5 × 800 meters at current 5K pace		24
10	7	6	2 × 3K or 2-mile LT intervals	–	10 × 100 meters	27
9	8	6	–	4 × 1K at 2–3 sec/lap slower than 5K goal pace	10 × 100 meters	30
8	7	6	4-mile tempo run	–	8 × 200 meters	27
7	8	7	–	4 × 1K at 1–2 sec/lap slower than 5K goal pace		30
6	9	7	3K or 2-mile time trial	–	8 × 200 meters	33
5	9	8	–	7 × 600 meters at 5K goal pace	10 × 100 meters	36
4	8	6	8K or 10K race	–	10 × 100 meters	33
3	8	7	–	5 × 1K at 5K goal pace	10 × 100 meters	33
2	8	6	3K or 2-mile race	–	8 × 200 meters	30
1	7	6	–	2 × 1,600 meters at 5K goal pace	10 × 100 meters	27
Race week	6	4	**Goal 5K race**	–	5 × 200 meters	24

5K Training Schedule
Schedule C: More than 40 miles/week

Weeks to goal	LR1	LR2	Lactate-threshold workouts	$\dot{V}O_2$max workouts	Basic speed workouts	Week's mileage	Per-centage of peak
11	8	7	–	6 × 800 meters at current 5K pace	12 × 100 meters	46	77
10	9	8	2 × 3K or 2-mile LT intervals	5 × 600 meters at current 5K pace		50	83
9	10	8	–	5 × 1K at 2–3 sec/lap slower than 5K goal pace	12 × 100 meters	54	90
8	9	8	4-mile tempo run	–	10 × 200 meters	50	83
7	10	8	–	5 × 1K at 1–2 sec/lap slower than 5K goal pace	12 × 100 meters	54	90
6	11	9	3K or 2-mile time trial	–	10 × 200 meters	58	97
5	11	10	–	2 × 2K at 1–2 sec/lap slower than 5K goal pace	12 × 100 meters	60	100
4	9	8	8K or 10K race	4 × 600 meters at 5K goal pace		54	90
3	10	9	–	5 × 1K at 5K goal pace	12 × 100 meters	54	90
2	9	8	3K or 2-mile race	–	8 × 200 meters	50	83
1	9	7	–	2 × 2K at 5K goal pace	12 × 100 meters	42	70
Race week	7	6	**Goal 5K race**	–	5 × 200 meters	36	60

CHAPTER 7

Training to Race 8K to 10K

© Victah

This chapter focuses on races of 8K (7 to 12 seconds short of 5 miles) to 10K. Although your pace during a 10K is a few seconds per mile slower than during an 8K, the two distances are grouped in this chapter because their physiological demands are almost identical.

Physiology of the 8K to 10K

The demands of races of 8K to 10K are interesting physiologically because a high lactate threshold and a high $\dot{V}O_2$max are equally important for racing success. You run 8Ks and 10Ks slightly above your lactate threshold, which means that your lactate levels rise slowly during the event. Besides having high $\dot{V}O_2$max values, the best racers at these distances have lactate thresholds that occur at a high percentage of their $\dot{V}O_2$maxes. Fortunately, you can increase both your $\dot{V}O_2$max and the percentage of your $\dot{V}O_2$max at which your lactate threshold occurs by designing your training specifically to stimulate these adaptations. The training schedules improve these physiological variables and thereby improve your racing performance.

Selecting Your Goal Pace

If you've raced an 8K or 10K before, you know roughly what your finishing time will be. Set realistic goals for your next race. Your race goal should be challenging yet achievable. For example, if you're preparing for your first race of the season, shoot for a solid performance rather than a personal best. Once you have run a couple of races, you should be ready to go after personal bests.

If you've never raced at these distances, or if you've run 8Ks and 10Ks but haven't focused on them, you can estimate your time by converting your times from other distances. Table 7.1 shows the conversion factors from 5K, 10K, 15K, 10 miles, 20K, half marathon, and marathon to the 8K or 5-mile. To predict your 8K or 5-mile time from your 5K, 10K, 15K, 10-mile, 20K, half-marathon, or marathon times, multiply the total number of seconds from your finishing times for those races by 1.66, .794, .513, .472, .375, .354, or .167, respectively. For example, if your 10-mile time is 60:00 (3,600 seconds), your predicted 8K time would be 1,699 seconds (3,600 × .472), or 28:19. For a table of equivalencies among distances, see the appendix.

Table 7.2 shows the conversion factors from 5K, 8K, 15K, 10 miles, half marathon, and marathon to the 10K. To predict your 10K time

Table 7.1   Conversion Factors to Estimate 8K or 5-Mile Time

5K	10K	15K	10 miles	20K	Half marathon	Marathon
1.66	.794	.513	.472	.375	.354	.167

Table 7.2   Conversion Factors to Estimate 10K Time

5K	8K-5 miles	15K	10 miles	20K	Half marathon	Marathon
2.09	1.26	.646	.594	.473	.445	.21

from your 5K, 8K, 15K, 10-mile, 20K, half-marathon, or marathon times, multiply the total number of seconds from your finishing times for those races by 2.09, 1.26, .646, .594, .473, .445, or .21, respectively. For example, if your half-marathon time is 1:20:00 (4,800 seconds), your predicted 10K time would be 2,136 seconds (4,800 × .445), or 35:36.

Training for the 8K to 10K

This chapter includes schedules for runners who typically train (a) less than 25 miles per week, (b) 25 to 45 miles per week, and (c) more than 45 miles per week. All the schedules are based on the physiological demands of these races. Your racing objective is to run as fast as you can for 8K or 10K. Your training objective is to increase your lactate threshold and your $\dot{V}O_2$max, so that you can run more quickly without accumulating high lactate levels.

Among the four types of training discussed in chapters 2 and 3, lactate threshold and $\dot{V}O_2$max training are most important for these distances, followed by pure endurance training. Basic speed, although not as important for these distances as for 5K racing, is the final arrow in your quiver. The 8K-10K schedules incorporate the priorities shown in table 7.3. Before the start of the schedule, several months before your goal race, you should concentrate your training on building endurance. Your highest priorities during that time should be pure endurance training and lactate-threshold training.

Elana Meyer

© Victah

10K Personal Record: 30:52
Career highlight at distance: 2nd, 1992 Olympic 10,000m
    Training and racing emphasis: Elana Meyer is one of the most complete runners in recent history—her PRs range from a 4:30 mile to a 2:25 marathon, with world road bests at 15K and the half marathon between the two ends. Nonetheless, she doesn't go about her training and racing randomly, just throwing together workouts and races in whatever way seems best on the day. Since becoming a marathoner in 1994, she has used a conventional buildup to a spring marathon as one of her focuses for the year, then recovered and emphasized world-class track racing in the summer and road races in the fall. She also takes advantage of her native South Africa's summer to get in some track races during January and February. She approaches 8K/10K races in two ways—as underdistance preparation for half marathons and spring marathons, and as the focus of a track season, which she then carries over to fall road races.

"I don't think you need megamiles to prepare for the 8K/10K races," she says. "You need faster workouts. My longest run in preparation for 8Ks and 10Ks is 60 to 90 minutes, and I will only push it up for marathon training."

When preparing for track races, Meyer does classic $\dot{V}O_2$max workouts, such as five one-kilometer repeats at 3,000m to 5,000m race pace, with a 400m jog between. When using 8K/10K races as part of her preparation for longer races, she favors longer, slightly slower workouts; one such session is alternating kilometers, which she runs in 3:00 to 3:10 (5K to 10K race pace), followed by one in 4:00 to 4:10, repeating the sequence five or six times.

Meyer likes to do workouts in which she varies the pace to combine several types of training in one session and to prepare her for the surges of world-class racing. In her strength phases, she does 1,600m at 5K race pace, 5K at marathon race pace, 1,600m at 5K to10K race pace, 5K at marathon race pace, finishing with 1,600m at 5K to 10K race pace. When peaking for a 10,000m on the track, she does a cut-down workout of six sets of 800m hard, 200m jog, then 300m hard. In the first set, she runs 2:40 for the 800m and :54 for the 300m, and works her way down to 2:15 and :46 by the end, to combine $\dot{V}O_2$max work with basic speed training.

7.3	Priorities for 8K-10K Training, in Order of Importance During the Schedule		
	Preschedule	First 6 weeks	Last 6 weeks
Basic speed	4	4	4
$\dot{V}O_2$max	3	1	1
Lactate threshold	2	1	2
Pure endurance	1	3	3

The base training schedules in chapter 4 will prepare you to start the schedules in this chapter.

During the first six weeks of the 8K-10K schedule, you'll continue to work on pure endurance, but lactate-threshold and $\dot{V}O_2$max training are the top priorities. During the last six weeks of the schedule, maintain endurance and emphasize $\dot{V}O_2$max and final preparations for your goal race.

Schedules Explained

The training schedules are 12 weeks long, which is enough time to provide a powerful stimulus to improve performance but not so long that you lose focus on your goal race. The schedules are organized vertically by the number of weeks until the race, so that your goal race is always your reference point. By looking down any one of the columns, you can easily see how the workouts progress during the 12 weeks for that type of training.

The schedules are also organized horizontally so that you can quickly view the key workouts for the week. In this way, you can see what the training emphasis is for the week, as well as see that you won't be doing too much in any week. The schedules don't recommend which days of the week to do which workout because that depends on the schedule that organizes the rest of your life.

Longest run   This is simply the longest run for the week. The schedules gradually increase your long run during the first six weeks to help prepare you for the endurance component of the race. For runners training more than 45 miles per week, the long run starts at 10 miles and increases to 13 miles. For runners training less than 25 miles per week, the long run starts at 7 miles and increases to 9 miles. Remember, long runs aren't jogs—to stimulate desirable physiological adaptations, such as increased capillary density, do your long runs 1:15 to 2:15 per mile slower than your 8K to 10K race pace.

Second longest run   The second longest run for the week reinforces the training adaptations of the long runs. These runs increase in distance in a similar pattern to the long runs.

Lactate-threshold workouts   The workouts in this column include tempo runs, LT intervals, time trials, and tune-up races. Chapter 3 explained tempo runs and LT intervals in detail. Tempo runs are continuous runs of 20 to 40 minutes at lactate-threshold pace. Lactate-threshold pace is approximately your 15K to half-marathon race pace. (For other ways to estimate lactate-threshold pace, see chapter 3.) For these workouts, warm up for about two miles, run the tempo run at lactate-threshold pace, and then cool down for a mile or two. Run LT intervals at the same pace as tempo runs but instead of one continuous run, break up the distance into two to four segments, with several minutes of slow running following each one.

Time trials and tune-up races are more intense than tempo runs or LT intervals. Time trials involve running as fast as you can in training for a given distance. They give you a good indication of how ready you are to race. Tune-up races are competitions that you enter as part of your buildup. Time trials and tune-up races serve the additional purpose of preparing you mentally for peak performance. During the 12 weeks, the lactate-threshold workouts progress from LT intervals and tempo runs to time trials and tune-up races. As you move through this progression, you more closely simulate the demands of your goal race.

Jon Brown

© Victah

10K Personal Record: 27:27
Career highlight at distance: 10th,
1996 Olympic 10,000m
    Training and racing emphasis:
Jon Brown is known and feared
among his peers as a meticulous
trainer who will be in the hunt in
the wide variety of races he contests. For most of his career he has
followed a traditional training pattern—cross-country races in the
winter, longer road races in the
spring, track in the summer, then
shorter road races in the fall. Since
making a 2:10 marathon debut in
the fall of 1997, he has extended
his range, but he still counts training for and racing 8K–10K races
as a vital part of his program. For
example, in 1997 he set his 10,000m
track personal record relatively
early in the season, then built on that base toward October's Chicago
Marathon. Once he recovered from Chicago, he immediately began to
run well in late-1997/early-1998 cross-country races in Europe at
distances of 10K to12K.

"My training doesn't really tend to differ much whether I'm pointing
toward cross-country, or 10K on the track or the roads," Brown says.
"You're training yourself to run for 20-odd minutes almost flat out. I do
a lot of threshold-type training—repeats of up to 15 minutes, slower
than 10K race pace, with short recoveries. I tend to do one of those
workouts a week, plus a 5K type workout on the track. In those, I'll do
a total of 12 to15 laps hard, at about 3K or 5K race pace. I might do 5
to 6 × a kilometer, or 8 × 800, or a workout of 2K, mile, 1200m, 800m,
400m. I don't do quarters much."

Brown rounds out his training with high-quality long runs. Most
weeks, his longest run is two hours, which he sometimes shortens to
1:45 in the summer.

$\dot{V}O_2$max workouts   These workouts are intervals of 600 meters to 2,000 meters. You can do these workouts on a track, a golf course, grass fields, trails, or uphill. As discussed in chapter 2, the most effective way to improve $\dot{V}O_2$max is to train at an intensity that requires 95 to 100 percent of your current $\dot{V}O_2$max. This is close to your 3K to 5K race pace, which is typically three to six seconds per lap faster than your 8K to 10K race pace. The schedules gradually increase the pace of these workouts to 5K goal pace as your fitness level improves. To recover between intervals, you should run slowly for a time of about 50 to 90 percent of the interval's duration.

Basic speed   The goal of these workouts is to improve your leg turnover and, in turn, your finishing speed. Although raw speed isn't essential for 8K to 10K racing, except at the world-class level, leg-turnover workouts will help maintain your basic speed and improve your running form.

Putting it all together   As an example of how to structure the week's training, look at nine weeks to go on Schedule B (25 to 45 miles per week). The schedule for that week includes four workouts. Add easy recovery runs or cross-training to reach the total of 35 miles for the week. (For how to equate cross-training with running mileage, see chapter 4.)

A typical way to complete that week's training is to do the longest run on Sunday, followed by a day off on Monday. Tuesday could be a recovery day consisting of an easy 5 miles. Wednesday would be time for a hard session, such as the $\dot{V}O_2$max workout. Thursday could be the second longest run, followed by a day off on Friday. The week could end with 10×100 meters as part of a 5-mile run on Saturday. You complete the 35 miles with five days of running, with the workouts evenly spaced throughout the week.

Avoid doing important workouts on consecutive days. If you have to do most of your hard running on the weekends, try to follow the two hard days with two easy days for recovery.

If you miss an important workout, don't try to make it up. For example, if injury, fatigue, bad weather, or the demands from the rest of your life put you behind schedule early in the week, don't run several hard sessions in a row to make up for lost time. The quality of your workouts will go down, and you'll increase your

Table 7.4	Properly Structuring a Sample Week From 8K-10K Schedule B
Sunday	10 miles
Monday	Off
Tuesday	5 miles
Wednesday	$\dot{V}O_2$max workout (8 miles, including warm-up, 5 × 2:30 uphill, and cool-down)
Thursday	7 miles
Friday	Off
Saturday	5 miles, including striders
Mileage for week	35

risk of injury. Instead, use the priorities outlined in table 7.3 to determine the most important sessions for where you are in the schedule. For example, say you're following Schedule B, and with five weeks to go before your goal race, you can fit in only two important workouts. According to table 7.3, your top training priorities among the workouts scheduled for that week are your $\dot{V}O_2$max and pure endurance. Therefore, you would do the 7 × 600-meter session listed as the week's $\dot{V}O_2$max workout on one day and the 10-miler listed as the week's longest run on another day.

Runners following Schedule C who want to do more than the weekly mileage listed in the schedule should follow the trend in mileage and simply adjust their mileage upward as a percentage of the prescribed mileage. For example, say that you want to reach a peak mileage of 80 per week; this would occur with six weeks to go. As noted in Schedule C, with one week to go, you should reach roughly 70 percent of your peak, or 56 miles (80 × 70 percent). Follow this principle throughout the program to ensure that your mileage builds in the first part of the schedule, then tapers as you approach your goal race.

© Victah

Races of 8K to 10K require a balance of aggressiveness and patience.

Racing Strategy and Mental Approach

These races require the aggressiveness of a 5K runner and the patience of a marathoner. As in the 5K, you can't afford to start slowly in an 8K or 10K. At the same time, if you go out too hard, you may experience a long, painful last three miles. The key to these races is to run good middle miles, when your mind has a tendency to drift. The first two miles of these races should be easy to run at your goal pace—you're still fresh and feeling good. Similarly, during the last mile, it's not difficult to rally your energy for a drive to the finish. But how you run in the middle miles largely determines your time for the race. Your mental approach should focus on these miles. Prepare yourself mentally to concentrate during this part of the race. Learn your mile splits and work to adhere to them.

8K to 10K Training Schedule
Schedule A: Less than 25 miles/week

Weeks to goal	LR1	LR2	Lactate-threshold workouts	$\dot{V}O_2$max workouts	Basic speed	Week's mileage
11	7	5	—	5 × 600 meters at current 5K pace	—	18
10	8	5	2 × 1 1/2-mile LT intervals	—	—	19
9	7	5	—	5 × 2:30 moderately steep uphill	—	20
8	8	6	3-mile tempo run	—	10 × 100 meters	21
7	8	6	—	6 × 2:30 moderately steep uphill	—	21
6	9	7	4-mile tempo run	—	10 × 100 meters	24
5	9	7	—	7 × 600 meters at 5K goal pace	—	24
4	8	6	2 1/2-mile time trial	—	10 × 100 meters	22
3	8	6	—	5 × 1K at 8K-10K goal pace	—	21
2	8	6	5K tune-up race	—	10 × 100 meters	21
1	7	5	—	2 × 1,600 meters at 1 sec/lap faster than 8K-10K goal pace	—	19
Race week	5	4	**Goal race**	—	4 × 300 meters	17

8K to 10K Training Schedule
Schedule B: 25–45 miles/week

Weeks to goal	LR1	LR2	Lactate-threshold workouts	$\dot{V}O_2max$ workouts	Basic speed	Week's mileage
11	8	6	–	5 × 800 meters at current 5K pace		28
10	9	7	2 × 2-mile LT intervals	–	10 × 100 meters	32
9	10	7	–	5 × 2:30 moderately steep uphill		35
8	9	7	4-mile tempo run	–	8 × 200 meters	34
7	10	8	–	6 × 2:30 moderately steep uphill	10 × 100 meters	38
6	11	8	2 1/2-mile time trial	–	10 × 100 meters	42
5	10	8	–	7 × 600 meters at 5K goal pace	10 × 100 meters	38
4	10	7	5K tune-up race	–	10 × 100 meters	35
3	10	8	–	5 × 1,200 meters at 1 sec/ lap slower than 8K-10K goal pace	10 × 100 meters	36
2	9	7	5K tune-up race	–	8 × 200 meters	33
1	9	7	–	2 × 1,600 meters at 1 sec/ lap faster than 8K-10K goal pace	10 × 100 meters	30
Race week	8	5	**Goal race**	–	5 × 300 meters	27

8K to 10K Training Schedule
Schedule C: More than 45 miles/week

Weeks to goal	LR1	LR2	Lactate-threshold workouts	V̇O₂max workouts	Basic speed	Week's mileage	Percentage of peak
11	10	8	–	6 × 800 meters at current 5K pace	12 × 100 meters	50	78
10	11	9	2 × 2-mile LT intervals	5 × 600 meters at current 5K pace	–	54	84
9	12	9	–	5 × 3:00 moderately steep uphill	12 × 100 meters	58	91
8	11	9	4-mile tempo run	–	12 × 100 meters	54	84
7	12	9	–	6 × 3:00 moderately steep uphill	12 × 100 meters	60	94
6	13	10	2 1/2-mile time trial	–	12 × 100 meters	64	100
5	12	10	–	5 × 1,200 at 1–2 sec/lap slower than 8K-10K goal pace	12 × 100 meters	62	97
4	11	9	5K tune-up race	4 × 600 meters at 5K goal pace		58	91
3	12	10	–	4 × 1,600 meters 8K-10K goal pace	12 × 100 meters	58	91
2	11	9	5K tune-up race	–	8 × 200 meters	54	84
1	10	8	–	2 × 2K at 1 sec/lap lap faster than 8K-10K goal pace	12 × 100 meters	46	72
Race week	8	6	**Goal race**	–	6 × 300 meters	40	62

CHAPTER 8

Training to Race 15K Through Half Marathon

© Victah

This chapter focuses on races of 15K (9.3 miles) to half marathon (13.1 miles), including races of 10 miles and 20K (12.4 miles). Although your pace during a half marathon is a few seconds per mile slower than during a 15K, this range of distances is grouped together because the physiological demands of these races are so similar.

Physiology of the 15K Through Half Marathon

In races of 15K through the half marathon, a high lactate threshold is more important for success than a high $\dot{V}O_2$max because you run these races at just about your lactate-threshold pace. The best racers at these distances have high lactate thresholds, which means that they don't start to accumulate lactate in their muscles and blood until they reach a high percentage of their $\dot{V}O_2$max. You can increase the percentage of your $\dot{V}O_2$max at which your lactate threshold occurs by designing your training specifically to stimulate this adaptation. With a properly designed schedule, increases in lactate threshold can occur for many years.

In races lasting more than an hour, glycogen depletion becomes a potential limiting factor in racing performance. As discussed in chapter 3, long runs deplete your glycogen stores, providing a stimulus for your muscles to store more glycogen. This positive adaptation will allow you to run farther before running low on glycogen. The training schedules in this chapter improve your lactate threshold, as well as your muscles' capacity to store glycogen, thereby improving your racing performance.

Selecting Your Goal Pace

If you've raced in the 15K to half-marathon range before, you know roughly what your finish time will be. Setting realistic goals for your next race can help keep you motivated during training. Your race goal should be challenging yet achievable. For example, if you're preparing for your first race of the season, shoot for a solid performance rather than a personal best. After you have completed a couple of shorter tune-up races, you should be ready to go after personal bests.

If you've never raced at these distances before, or have not focused on races of these distances in your training, you can estimate your time by converting your racing times from other distances. Table 8.1 shows the conversion factors from 5K, 8K, 10K, 10 miles, 20K, half

Anne Marie Lauck

© Victah

15K Personal Record: 48:43
Career highlight at distance: U.S. Champion at half marathon, 1996
Training and racing emphasis: Anne Marie Lauck has long had a reputation as a ferocious trainer and, in races, a fearless frontrunner. These qualities suit her well in 15K-half-marathon races—her training nicely blends speed and endurance, and her aggressiveness in races keeps her competitive when, as she says, "These days, people run 10-milers and half marathons like 10Ks, so you can't usually count on coming from behind." That's not to suggest that Lauck's training and racing is based solely on running as much as possible as quickly as possible. Such an approach wouldn't have allowed her to win the USA Running Circuit in 1996, nor to place 10th in the Olympic Marathon that year. Lauck mixes race distances throughout the year—even when preparing for a marathon, she doesn't neglect 5Ks. She runs 15K-half marathons both as early-spring tests of her base-training fitness, and as integral tune-ups before a marathon. In both cases, Lauck stresses completeness in her training—in addition to long runs, she does $\dot{V}O_2$ max workouts, such as 8 X 800m at 5K race pace, tempo runs to boost her lactate threshold, and regular basic speed sessions. "Even in the middle of the winter," she says, "I try not to ignore my leg turnover. I'll do something like 12 X 200m, not as fast as I would when peaking for a track race, but still pretty hard."

Lauck thinks that 15K-half marathons deserve respect because of the balance between distance and speed that they require. "When you're well prepared for one, you can run them close to what you can run for shorter races, so they're exciting," she says, "but they're also long enough that you know you've accomplished something more than running another 10K. Because you're running so far at such a good clip, you should limit your efforts at these distances. Don't run one every month; pick one and really focus on it."

Table 8.1   Conversion Factors to Estimate 15K, 10-Mile (10M), 20K, and Half-Marathon Times

	5K	8K	10K	15K	10M	20K	Half marathon	Marathon
15K	3.24	1.95	1.55	NA	.92	.73	.69	.325
10M	3.52	2.12	1.68	1.09	NA	.796	.75	.354
20K	4.42	2.66	2.12	1.37	1.26	NA	.937	.445
Half marathon	4.69	2.83	2.24	1.45	1.33	1.07	NA	.472

marathon, and marathon to 15K, 10 miles, 20K, and half marathon. For example, if your 10K time is 40:00 (2,400 seconds), your predicted half-marathon time would be 5,376 seconds (2,400 × 2:24) or 1:29:36. For a table of equivalencies among distances, see the appendix.

Training for the 15K Through Half Marathon

This chapter includes schedules for runners who typically train (a) less than 30 miles per week, (b) 30 to 50 miles per week, and (c) more than 50 miles per week. Regardless of your training mileage, the schedules are based on the physiological demands of these races. Your racing objective is to run as fast as you can for 15K, 10 miles, 20K, or the half marathon. Your primary training objective is to increase your lactate threshold, so that you can run faster without accumulating high lactate levels.

The 15K through half-marathon schedules were developed according to the priorities shown in table 8.2. Among the four types of training discussed in chapters 2 and 3, lactate-threshold training is most important for these distances, followed by pure endurance training, $\dot{V}O_2$max training and, finally, basic speed. The schedules assume that you are starting with a basic level of fitness. Before the start of the schedule, when your goal race is still months away, you should concentrate on building endurance. Your highest priorities during that time should be pure endurance training and lactate-threshold training. The base training schedules in chapter 4 will prepare you to start the schedules in this chapter.

8.2	Priorities for 15K Through Half-Marathon Training, in Order of Importance During the Schedule		
	Preschedule	First 9 weeks	Last 6 weeks
Basic speed	4	4	4
$\dot{V}O_2$max	3	3	2
Lactate threshold	2	1	1
Pure endurance	1	2	3

During the 15 weeks of the 15K through half-marathon schedules, lactate-threshold training is the top priority. During the first 9 weeks of the schedules, you improve pure endurance; $\dot{V}O_2$max is the third priority. During the last 6 weeks of the schedules, you maintain pure endurance and place slightly more emphasis on $\dot{V}O_2$max training.

Schedules Explained

The training schedules are 15 weeks long, which is ample time to provide a powerful stimulus to improve performance. Fifteen weeks is a long time to prepare for one race, and if you're not used to developing your training for a specific goal, you may find it difficult to stay focused on your goal race. But if you've chosen a race in this range as your target, you probably know that there are no instant lottery winners in distance running. The schedules are organized vertically by the number of weeks until the race, so that your goal race is always your reference point. By looking down any one of the columns, you can easily see how the workouts progress during the 15 weeks for that type of training.

The schedules are also organized horizontally so that you can quickly view the key workouts for the week. In this way, it's easy to get a feel for the types of training stimuli being emphasized that week. You can also see that you won't have to do too much in any week. The schedules don't recommend which days of the week to do which workout; that depends of the schedule that organizes the rest of your life.

Longest run   During the first nine weeks the schedules gradually increase your longest run for the week to help prepare you for the endurance component of the race. For runners training more than 50 miles per week, the long run starts at 12 miles and increases to 17 miles. For runners training less than 30 miles per week, the long run starts at 8 miles and increases to 13 miles. Remember, long runs aren't jogs. To stimulate desirable physiological adaptations, such as increased capillary density, you should do your long runs one to two minutes per mile slower than your 15K to half-marathon race pace.

Second longest run   The purpose of the second longest run for the week is to reinforce the training adaptations of the long runs. These runs increase in distance in a similar pattern to the long runs. These workouts are more important for races of 15K to the half marathon than they are for shorter races. You should do the second long run at a similar pace to, or slightly faster than, the long run. If your races will be in hilly terrain, try to simulate race conditions in selecting where to do these runs.

Lactate-threshold workouts   The workouts in this column include tempo runs, LT intervals, time trials, and tune-up races. Tempo runs and LT intervals were explained in detail in chapter 3. Tempo runs are continuous runs of 20 to 40 minutes at lactate-threshold pace. Lactate-threshold pace is approximately your 15K to half-marathon race pace. (For other ways to estimate lactate-threshold pace, see chapter 3.) For these workouts, warm up for about two miles, run the tempo run at lactate-threshold pace, and then cool down for a mile or two. Run LT intervals at the same pace as tempo runs but instead of one continuous run, break up the distance into two to four segments, with several minutes of slow running after each segment.

Time trials and tune-up races are more intense than tempo runs or LT intervals. Time trials involve running as fast as you can in training for a given distance. They give you a good indication of how ready you are to race. Tune-up races are competitions that you enter as part of your buildup. Time trials and tune-up races serve the additional purpose of preparing you mentally for peak performance. During the 15 weeks, the lactate-threshold workouts progress from LT intervals and tempo runs to time trials and tune-up races. As you move through this progression, you more closely simulate the demands of your goal race. Lactate-threshold workouts also help prepare you mentally for your goal race, because you do these workouts at your 15K to half-marathon race pace.

Todd Williams

© Victah

15K Personal Record: 42:22
Career highlight at distance: 4-time national 15K champion
Training and racing emphasis: Todd Williams has been touted as the next great American marathoner. In part that's because even when 10,000m on the track was his main focus, he ran exceptionally well when dabbling in longer road races. Now that he's a marathoner, debuting with a 2:11 in Chicago in 1997, he plans to emphasize 15K/half marathons races more.

Williams' reputation as an adept 15K/half-marathon runner stems mostly from his annual appearance at March's Gate River Run 15K, in Jacksonville, FL, which has served as the national championship for the distance for the last several years. Williams has won the race every year since 1994 except once, and in 1995 he set an American best for the distance there. (He has also won a national championship at 10 miles and, on an aided course in Tokyo, just missed breaking one hour for a half marathon.) "I divide my year into quarters, just like Uncle Sam," Williams says. "A 15K at that time of the year is a good barometer to see where I'm at."

Williams' early-year training is well-balanced—it includes short indoor track races, basic speed sessions, $\dot{V}O_2$max workouts, threshold training, and high-quality distance runs on the roads. "The big key to doing well in these races is staying healthy so that you can run the miles with a mix of tempo and speed workouts," Williams says. During his buildup to the Jacksonville race, he tries to average 110 miles per week; the only time during the year that he runs more is when building toward a fall marathon.

Williams counts workouts of 300m and 400m as basic speed sessions. "Before setting the record in 1995," he says, "one of my workouts was 15 × 300 in :45, with :35 rest between. I'll also do 12 quarters in :62." Williams prefers to break his lactate-threshold into repeats with short rest, such as three 2-mile repeats at roughly 15K race pace, with 3 to 4 minutes between.

$\dot{V}O_2$max workouts   These are intervals of 600 meters to 2,000 meters. You can run these workouts on a track, golf course, grass fields, trails, or uphill. As discussed in chapter 2, the greatest stimulus to improve $\dot{V}O_2$max is to train at an intensity that requires 95 to 100 percent of your current $\dot{V}O_2$max. This corresponds to about your 3K to 5K race pace, which is typically 5 to 10 seconds per lap faster than your 15K to half-marathon race pace. The schedules gradually increase the pace of these workouts to 5K goal pace as your fitness level improves. To recover between intervals, run slowly for a time that lasts 50 to 90 percent of the duration of the interval.

Basic speed   These workouts will improve your leg turnover. They'll help maintain the basic leg speed that you'll need for shorter races.

Putting it all together   As an example of how to structure the week's training, look at 11 weeks to go on Schedule B (30 to 50 miles per week). That week includes three workouts. Add easy recovery runs or cross-training as necessary to reach the total of 39 miles for the week. (For how to equate cross-training with running mileage, see chapter 4.)

A typical way to complete that week's training is to do the longest run on Sunday, followed by a day off on Monday. Tuesday could be a recovery day consisting of an easy 6 miles. Wednesday would be time for the $\dot{V}O_2$max workout. Thursday could be the second longest run, followed by a day off on Friday. The week could end with a 6-mile run on Saturday. You would complete 39 miles in five days of running, with the workouts evenly spaced throughout the week.

Avoid doing important workouts on consecutive days. If you have to get most of your hard running in on the weekends, try to follow the two hard days with two easy days for recovery.

If you miss an important workout, don't try to make it up. If injury, fatigue, bad weather, or the demands from the rest of your life put you behind schedule early in the week, don't run several hard sessions in a row to make up for lost time. If you try to squeeze several hard sessions together, the quality of your workouts will go down and you'll increase your risk of injury. Instead, use the priorities outlined in table 8.2 to determine the most important sessions for where you are in the schedule. For example, say you're following Schedule B and with six weeks to go you can fit in only two important workouts.

Table 8.3	Properly Structuring a Sample Week From 15K through Half-Marathon Schedule B
Sunday	12 miles
Monday	Off
Tuesday	6 miles
Wednesday	$\dot{V}O_2$max workout (7 miles, including warm-up, 5 × 2:30 uphill, and cool-down)
Thursday	8 miles
Friday	Off
Saturday	6 miles
Mileage for week	39

According to table 8.2, your top training priorities among the workouts scheduled for that week are developing your lactate threshold, increasing your $\dot{V}O_2$max, and developing your pure endurance, respectively. You'll note on Schedule B for that week (see page 143) there is no $\dot{V}O_2$max workout scheduled, but there is both a lactate-threshold and an endurance workout. Therefore, you would do the 4-mile time trial listed as the week's lactate-threshold workout on one day and the 15-miler listed as the week's longest run on another day.

Runners following Schedule C who want to do more than the weekly mileage listed in the schedule should follow the trend in mileage outlined, and simply adjust their mileage upward as a percentage of the prescribed mileage. For example, say that you want to reach a peak mileage of 85 per week; this would occur with six weeks to go. As noted in Schedule C, with one week to go, your mileage should be roughly 75 percent of your peak, or 63 miles (85 × 75 percent). Follow this principle throughout the program to ensure that your mileage builds in the first part of the schedule, then tapers as you approach your goal race.

Racing Strategy and Mental Approach

These races require mental toughness. The pace is right at your lactate threshold, yet you must hold this pace for 9.3 to 13.1 miles.

© Victah

Proper pacing and hydration are two important elements of success in races of 15K through the half marathon.

Although every race requires a balance of aggressiveness and pa-tience, in races of 15K or longer the scale tips toward discretion in the early stages. By starting the race fast, you may gain a few seconds per mile in the early stages of the race. Going out too hard is dangerous, however, because it can lead to a slow last few miles and may ultimately add several minutes to your finishing time. The key to these races is to run an even pace, particularly in the second half of the race. By slowing less in the second half of the race, you will better your time.

You can build mental toughness during training. Try to run your lactate-threshold and $\dot{V}O_2$max workouts evenly. Practice holding the pace as you fatigue. Similarly, during your long runs, don't slow in the final miles. Gradually increase the effort as your long runs progress so that you maintain an even pace. This preparation will be invaluable on race day against less-prepared opponents.

15K through Half-Marathon Training Schedule
Schedule A: Less than 30 miles/week

Weeks to goal	LR1	LR2	Lactate-threshold workouts	VO₂max workouts	Basic speed	Week's mileage
14	8	6	–	–	–	20
13	9	6	–	5 × 2:00 on grass, golf course, or trails	–	21
12	9	6	2 × 1 1/2-mile LT intervals	–	–	22
11	10	7	–	5 × 2:30 moderately steep uphill	–	24
10	10	7	2 × 2-mile LT intervals	–	8 × 100 meters	24
9	11	8	–	5 × 3:30 moderately steep uphill	–	26
8	12	–	8-mile run with long hills or 3-mile tempo run	–	8 × 100 meters	26

15K through Half-Marathon Training Schedule
Schedule A: Less than 30 miles/week

Weeks to goal	LR1	LR2	Lactate-threshold workouts	$\dot{V}O_2$max workouts	Basic speed	Week's mileage
7	11	8	–	5 × 3:30 moderately steep uphill	–	28
6	13	9	4-mile tempo run	–	8 × 100 meters	30
5	12	9	–	4 × 1,200 meters at 2 sec/lap slower than 8K-10K goal pace	–	30
4	10	8	4-mile time trial	–	8 × 100 meters	28
3	11	8	–	3 × 1,600 at 1 sec/lap slower than 8K-10K goal pace	–	26
2	11	6	8K-10K tune-up race	–	8 × 100 meters	26
1	8	6	–	3 × 1,600 meters at 8K-10K goal pace	–	24
Race week	6	4	**Goal race**	–	8 × 100 meters	22

15K through Half-Marathon Training Schedule
Schedule B: 30–50 miles/week

Weeks to goal	LR1	LR2	Lactate-threshold workouts	$\dot{V}O_2$max workouts	Basic speed	Week's mileage
14	10	7	2 × 1 1/2-mile LT intervals	–	–	30
13	11	7	–	5 × 2:30 on grass, golf course, or trails	–	33
12	11	7	2 × 2-mile LT intervals	–	8 × 100 meters	36
11	12	8	–	5 × 2:30 moderately steep uphill	–	39
10	12	8	8-mile run with long hills or 3-mile tempo run	–	10 × 100 meters	39
9	13	8	–	5 × 3:00 moderately steep uphill	–	42
8	14	9	4-mile tempo run	–	10 × 100 meters	42

15K through Half-Marathon Training Schedule
Schedule B: 30–50 miles/week

Weeks to goal	LR1	LR2	Lactate-threshold workouts	V̇O₂max workouts	Basic speed	Week's mileage
7	13	9	–	5 × 3:30 moderately steep uphill	–	46
6	15	10	4-mile time trial	–	10 × 100 meters	50
5	13	10	–	5 × 1,200 meters at 2 sec/lap slower than 8K-10K goal pace	–	50
4	11	8	8K or 10K tune-up race	–	10 × 100 meters	44
3	14	9	–	4 × 1,600 meters at 1 sec/lap slower than 8K-10K goal pace	–	44
2	12	8	8K or 10K tune-up race	–	10 × 100 meters	42
1	10	7	–	3 × 1,600 meters at 8K-10K goal pace	–	38
Race week	8	5	**Goal race**	–	8 × 100 meters	32

15K through Half-Marathon Training Schedule
Schedule C: More than 50 miles/week

Weeks to goal	LR1	LR2	Lactate-threshold workouts	$\dot{V}O_2$max workouts	Basic speed	Week's mileage	Per-centage of peak
14	12	9	2 × 2-mile LT intervals	—	—	50	70
13	13	9	—	5 × 3:00 on grass, golf course, or trails	—	54	75
12	13	9	2 × 2 1/2-mile LT intervals	—	8 × 100 meters	58	81
11	14	10	—	5 × 2:30 moderately steep uphill	—	58	81
10	14	10	10-mile run with long hills or 4-mile tempo run	—	10 × 100 meters	62	86
9	15	10	—	5 × 3:00 moderately steep uphill		66	92
8	16	11	5-mile tempo run	—	12 × 100 meters	62	86

144

15K through Half-Marathon Training Schedule
Schedule C: More than 50 miles/week

Weeks to goal	LR1	LR2	Lactate-threshold workouts	$\dot{V}O_2$max workouts	Basic speed	Week's mileage	Per-centage of peak
7	15	11	–	5 × 4:00 moderately steep uphill	–	68	94
6	17	12	4-mile time trial	–	12 × 100 meters	72	100
5	15	12	–	5 × 1,200 meters at 2 sec/lap slower than 8K-10K goal pace	–	70	97
4	13	10	8K or 10K tune-up race	–	12 × 100 meters	62	86
3	16	11	–	4 × 1,600 meters at 1 sec/lap slower than 8K-10K goal pace	12 × 100 meters	64	89
2	14	10	8K or 10K tune-up race	–	12 × 100 meters	60	83
1	12	9	–	3 × 2K at 8K-10K goal pace	–	54	75
Race week	9	7	**Goal race**	–	8 × 100 meters	44	61

CHAPTER 9

Training for the Marathon

© Victah

This chapter focuses on the marathon, the most respected and most analyzed race in running. Unfortunately, much of what has been written about the marathon is based on folk wisdom rather than physiology. Yet the physiology of the event is straightforward—the marathon is a test of stamina, even when your confidence at the distance has increased to where you're trying to shave seconds from your personal best. If you're motivated enough to follow the schedules in this chapter, you'll improve your marathon time and the consistency of your performances.

Physiology of the Marathon

The marathon requires lots of pure endurance, the ability to store a large quantity of glycogen in your muscles, and a high lactate threshold. With the right balance of training, your body will adapt and improve in all these attributes.

Improvement in pure endurance was discussed in detail in chapter 3. Two of the main adaptations to pure endurance training are increased capillary density and increased ability to use free fatty acids—to burn more fat relative to carbohydrate at a given running speed. The result is that glycogen, the stored form of carbohydrates in your muscles, is spared. This permits you to run farther before depleting your stores. This is important in the marathon because glycogen availability is a limiting factor in performance.

Another important adaptation to pure endurance training is increased glycogen storage. As discussed in chapter 3, long runs deplete your glycogen stores, providing a stimulus for your muscles to store more glycogen. By increasing the distance of your long runs and, secondarily, your weekly mileage, you gradually increase the capacity of your muscles to store glycogen. Because of the risk of injury, you shouldn't increase your long runs or mileage too quickly. The schedules in this chapter increase the long runs and weekly mileage according to an aggressive yet achievable progression.

The ability to improve on marathon performances also requires a high lactate threshold, meaning that lactate doesn't start to accumulate in your muscles and blood until you reach a high percentage of your $\dot{V}O_2$max. You can increase the percentage of your $\dot{V}O_2$max at

Tegla Loroupe

© Victah

Marathon Personal Record: 2:20:47

Career highlight at distance: World record, 1998 Rotterdam Marathon

Training and racing emphasis: Tegla Loroupe is the fastest female marathoner in history. However, her talent is such that she has also been competitive at a world-class level at races as short as 3,000m. Above all, Loroupe simply seems to love racing—even with a spring and a fall marathon on her schedule, she competes as many as 25 times per year.

Since making her marathon debut with a win at New York City in 1994, Loroupe has followed a conventional pattern for her year: During the winter, she runs cross-country races and at least one half marathon as preludes to a spring marathon. After recovering from that effort, she runs road races in Europe and the US, usually in the 10K range, then hits the European track circuit for 5,000m and 10,000m contests. Longer road races in the fall serve as a bridge between the shorter races of the summer and a fall marathon.

Loroupe doesn't say much about her training. Before setting the world record at the 1998 Rotterdam Marathon, she averaged more than 100 miles per week, and twice hit 130-mile weeks. She does long runs of up to 2.5 hours over hilly terrain, even when training for flat-course marathons. Prior to her marathons, Loroupe does runs of 12K-21K at her goal pace, and includes regular sessions of kilometer repeats at $\dot{V}O_2$max pace. Her frequent shorter races serve as high-quality $\dot{V}O_2$max and lactate-threshold workouts throughout the year.

which your lactate threshold occurs by designing your training specifically to stimulate this adaptation. With a properly designed schedule, you can achieve increases in lactate threshold for many years.

The training schedules in this chapter provide a powerful stimulus to improve your pure endurance, your muscles' capacity to store glycogen, and your lactate threshold, thereby improving your performance in the marathon. These adaptations, although predictable, occur over time. Marathoners aren't made overnight. Runners become marathoners with intelligent and consistent training.

Selecting Your Goal Pace

If you've run a marathon before, you know roughly what your finish time will be. Setting realistic goals for your next marathon can help keep you motivated during training. Your goal should be challenging yet achievable.

If you've never raced at this distance before, you can estimate your marathon time by converting your racing times from other distances. Table 9.1 presents conversion factors from other standard road-race distances to the marathon for experienced marathoners. For a table of equivalencies among distances, see the appendix.

Be warned, however, that predicting marathon times is more art than science. There's great variability between runners in the ability

Table 9.1   Conversion Factors to Estimate Marathon Times

	Marathon
8K	5.99
10K	4.76
15K	3.07
10 miles	2.82
20K	2.25
Half marathon	2.12

to move up in distance; runners with equal 10K times aren't equally adept at the marathon. And if you're running your first marathon, these conversions will be too aggressive. It's better to err on the side of caution when running your first marathon.

Training for the Marathon

This chapter includes schedules for runners who typically train (a) less than 40 miles per week, (b) 40 to 60 miles per week, and (c) more than 60 miles per week. All schedules are based on the physiological demands of the marathon. Your racing objective is to maintain as fast a pace as you can for 26.2 miles. Achieving this objective requires improving your pure endurance, your muscles' capacity to store glycogen, and your lactate threshold so that you slow as little as possible during the race.

The marathon schedules were developed according to the priorities shown in table 9.2. Among the four types of training discussed in chapters 2 and 3, pure endurance training and lactate-threshold training are most important for the marathon, followed by $\dot{V}O_2$max training, then basic speed. The schedules assume that you're starting with a basic level of fitness. Before the start of the schedule, when your goal marathon is several months away, you should concentrate on building endurance. Pure endurance training should be your highest priority during that time. The base training schedules in chapter 4 will prepare you to start the schedules in this chapter. During the 18 weeks of the marathon schedules, the top priority gradually shifts from pure endurance training to lactate-threshold training.

9.2	Priorities for Marathon Training, in Order of Importance During the Schedule		
	Preschedule	First 12 weeks	Last 6 weeks
Basic speed	4	4	4
$\dot{V}O_2$max	3	3	3
Lactate threshold	2	2	1
Pure endurance	1	1	2

Schedules Explained

The training schedules are 18 weeks long, which is enough time to provide a strong stimulus to improve your marathon performance. Eighteen weeks is a long time to prepare for one race. If you're not used to training for a specific goal, you may find it difficult to stay focused on your goal race. The marathon, however, requires your respect; it's worth an 18-week investment in hard work to improve your marathon performance. The schedules are organized vertically by the number of weeks until the race, so that your goal race is always your reference point. By looking down any of the columns, you can see how the workouts progress during the 18 weeks for that type of training.

The schedules are also organized horizontally, so that you can view the key workouts for the week. In this way, you can see the types of training stimuli being emphasized that week. You can also see that you don't have to do too much in any week. The schedules don't recommend which days of the week to do which workout because that depends on other schedules in your life.

The exception is during the last three weeks. Because of the importance of tapering—reducing mileage and intensity to prepare your body for a peak effort—before a marathon, the schedules give a day-by-day guide to maximizing the effectiveness of the taper. For more on tapering, see chapter 5.

Longest run   The schedules gradually increase your long run to help prepare you for the all-important endurance component of the race. For runners training more than 60 miles per week, the long run starts at 15 miles and increases to 22 miles. For runners training less than 40 miles per week, the long run starts at 11 miles and increases to 20 miles. Although this is a substantial increase in the first 14 weeks of the schedules, it's important physiologically and psychologically to complete a 20-mile run before running a marathon. Remember, long runs aren't jogs. To stimulate the physiological adaptations that are crucial to marathon success, such as increased capillary density and increased glycogen storage, do your long runs 0:45 to 1:30 per mile slower than your marathon race pace.

Second longest run   The purpose of the second longest run is to reinforce the training adaptations of the long runs. These runs

Jerry Lawson

© Human Kinetics

Marathon Personal Record: 2:09:35
Career highlight at distance: American record, 1997 Chicago Marathon
Training and racing emphasis: Jerry Lawson bases his running on trying to produce two strong marathons per year, one in the spring and one in the fall. His devotion to the marathon has paid off—at the 1996 Chicago, he placed second in 2:10:04, which tied him for the American record on a loop course, and in 1997, he took sole possession of the record with a 2:09:35.

Even with his marathon focus, Lawson is careful not to ignore other aspects of balanced running. For example, early in 1998 he settled briefly in New Zealand and trained to break 4:00 for the mile. Says Lawson, "My focus with going for the mile was to build the 'pure speed' and then keep shifting the focus and moving up in distance to prepare myself for a solid 10,000m and then carry it to the fall for a tremendous marathon." Although he didn't break 4:00 in his one attempt, he "managed to run a 1:54 for 800m on a windy day in mid-January," Lawson says.

Building up to a marathon, however, Lawson, with the guidance of Jack Daniels, emphasizes boosting his endurance and lactate threshold. Indeed, Lawson is legendary in some circles for his high mileage—he has put in a 210-mile week, and one August, he ran 834 miles (an average of almost 27 miles per day). But to prepare to race the marathon, he does more than log miles. An integral part of his planning with Daniels involves structuring lactate-threshold workouts and having the confidence to rest in the last few weeks before the race.

Before setting the American record in 1997, "I did numerous workouts of two-mile intervals with two minutes rest, sometimes running three repeats, sometimes running four," Lawson says. He

→

aimed to run these workouts at :72 per lap, which, at about 4:50 per mile, is roughly his half-marathon race pace. "My training was geared at getting my endurance and strength up to a point where the pace wouldn't be a problem," Lawson says. These workouts are examples of the "cruise intervals" discussed in chapter 3 that Daniels has popularized—running long repeats at lactate-threshold pace with short rests between the intervals. As one of his key workouts before Chicago, Lawson ran three miles in 14:27, left the track for a moderately paced 10-miler, then returned to the track to run three one-mile repeats at LT pace, with a one-minute rest between intervals.

increase in distance in a similar pattern to, and should be run at a similar pace to, your long runs. Schedule C includes a special workout six weeks before the marathon. This is a 14-mile run in which you run the last 2 miles at half-marathon race pace, preferably on an accurately measured stretch of road or on a track. This workout increases your ability to finish your marathon strongly.

Lactate-threshold workouts   The workouts in this column include tempo runs, LT intervals, and tune-up races. Tempo runs and LT intervals were explained in detail in chapter 3. Tempo runs are continuous runs of 20 to 40 minutes at lactate-threshold pace. Lactate-threshold pace is approximately your 15K to half-marathon race pace. (For other ways to estimate lactate-threshold pace, see chapter 3.) For these workouts, warm up for about two miles, run the tempo run at lactate-threshold pace, and then cool down for a mile or two. Run LT intervals at the same pace as tempo runs but instead of one continuous run, break up the distance into two to four segments, with several minutes of slow running after each.

Tune-up races are more intense than tempo runs or LT intervals. These are competitions that you enter as part of your buildup. During the 18 weeks, the lactate-threshold workouts progress from LT intervals to tempo runs to tune-up races. This sequence builds to a close simulation of the demands of the marathon. Lactate-threshold workouts will also help you prepare mentally for the marathon.

$\dot{V}O_2$max workouts   These workouts are intervals of 600 meters to 2,000 meters. You can run these workouts on a track, golf course, grass fields, trails, or uphill. As discussed in chapter 2, the greatest stimulus to improve $\dot{V}O_2$max is to train at an intensity that requires 95 to 100 percent of your current $\dot{V}O_2$max. This corresponds to about your 3K to 5K race pace. Recover by running slowly for a time that lasts 50 to 90 percent of the duration of the interval.

Basic speed These workouts will improve your leg turnover. They'll help you to maintain your basic leg speed for shorter races.

Putting it all together As an example of how to structure the week's training, look at 12 weeks to go on Schedule B (40 to 60 miles per week). The schedule for that week includes three workouts. Add easy recovery runs or cross-training as necessary to reach the total of 50 miles for the week (see table 9.3). For how to equate cross-training with running mileage, see chapter 4.

A typical way to complete this week's training is to do the longest run on Sunday, followed by a day off on Monday. Tuesday could be a recovery day consisting of an easy 6 miles. Wednesday would be time for a hard session, such as the LT intervals. Thursday's run could be 5 miles, followed by the second longest run on Friday. The week could end with an easy 4-miler on Saturday. You would complete the 50 miles in 6 days of running, with the workouts evenly spaced throughout the week.

Avoid doing important workouts on consecutive days. If your personal schedule requires that you do most of your hard running on

Table 9.3	Properly Structuring a Sample Week From Marathon Schedule B
Sunday	17 miles
Monday	Off
Tuesday	6 miles
Wednesday	LT intervals (8 miles, including warm-up, 2 × 2-miles at LT pace, and cool-down)
Thursday	5 miles
Friday	10 miles
Saturday	4 miles
Mileage for week	50

the weekends, try to follow the two hard days with two easy days for recovery.

If you miss an important workout, don't try to make it up. If injury, fatigue, bad weather, or the demands from the rest of your life put you behind schedule early in the week, don't run several hard sessions in a row to make up for lost time. Doing so will reduce the quality of your workouts, and you'll increase your risk of injury. Instead, use the priorities outlined in table 9.2 to determine the most important sessions for where you are in the schedule. Say you're following Schedule B and with seven weeks to go you can fit in only two important workouts. According to table 9.2, your top training priorities among the workouts scheduled for that week are developing your pure endurance and lactate threshold. Therefore, you would do the 15-miler listed as the week's longest run on one day and the 6-mile tempo run listed as the week's lactate-threshold workout on another day.

Last three weeks   As discussed in chapter 5, tapering for the three weeks before your marathon will maximize the benefits of your training. Because many runners overdo it during this crucial period, the marathon schedules, unlike those for other race distances, give daily workouts. Here are some general guidelines to flesh out the schedules.

In the week that ends two weeks before your marathon, you should run about 80 percent of your peak mileage. This is the week in which many marathoners do too much. Unfortunately, if you overtrain during this week, it's hard to recover adequately before your marathon. The last long run, done two weeks before the marathon, strikes a balance between being long enough to remind you that you're a marathoner and short enough not to interfere with tapering.

In the week that ends one week before your marathon, you should run about 60 percent of your peak mileage. The 11- to 13-miler done with a week to go is the last piece of distance work. It will remind your mind and body that you're well trained. By now, you will be starting to feel smooth and powerful.

During the last six days before your marathon, you should run about one-third of your peak mileage. For example, Schedule

B runners who peaked at 60 miles should run 20 miles between Monday and Saturday before the marathon. During
this last week, try to run at approximately the same time of day
you will run the marathon. The human body likes routine. It
programs itself to run at the same time each day. By training at
the time of day when you will run the marathon, you can
help prepare your digestive system, your energy systems, and
even your mental energy to operate at peak efficiency for the
race.

Wednesday's workout is your secret weapon—the dress rehearsal
for the marathon. Put on your racing gear, shoes and all. Warm up for
10 to 20 minutes, run two to three miles at marathon race pace, then
cool down for 10 to 15 minutes. This run helps shake loose your
mental and physical cobwebs. Most marathoners find this session to
be a great confidence booster. During this run, you should feel light
on your feet and ready for the marathon. If you notice any muscle
tightness or general fatigue, you still have time to get a massage and
rest.

As discussed in chapter 5, during the last three days before the
marathon you should increase your complex-carbohydrate intake. You should drink a lot of liquid during this time but stay
away from alcohol and caffeine, which are diuretics that will
dehydrate you.

Runners following Schedule C who want to do more than the
weekly mileage listed in the schedule should follow the trend in
mileage outlined and simply adjust their mileage upward as a
percentage of the prescribed mileage. For example, say that you want
to reach a peak mileage of 100 per week; this would occur with five
weeks to go. As noted in Schedule C, with one week to go, you should
be at roughly 60 percent of your peak, or 60 miles (100 × 60 percent).
Follow this principle throughout the program to build your mileage
in the first part of the schedule and taper as you approach your
marathon.

Racing Strategy and Mental Approach

Marathon running is a gamble. As the last four Olympic marathons have shown, even the best marathoners in the world
can't be certain of consistently top performances. But even though

it's impossible to guarantee success in the marathon, you can tilt the odds in your favor with the right preparation. You do much of this preparation before you reach the starting line. Attention to details in the last few days before the race, such as carbohydrate loading, hydration, and tapering, increases your likelihood of success.

During the marathon, the most effective racing strategy is simple: Be patient. For every minute you gain through exuberance in the first half of the race, you usually hand back several during the second. How can you minimize both your finishing time and your chances of blowing up? Realize that the most efficient way to use your body's energy supply is to run close to an even pace. By holding back during the early miles, you'll conserve your glycogen reserves for later in the race.

The most effective mental approach for the marathon is also simple. During the first half, run comfortably and prepare mentally for the second half. Whether you aspire to a 2:10 marathon or a 4:10,

© Human Kinetics

Success in the marathon requires intelligence in your training as well as on race day.

it's wise to shepherd your resources for the second half of the race. That requires discipline during the early miles, when your legs feel fresh and the pace feels slow. Be assured that you'll need your mental energy for the last miles of the race, when your muscles will complain and your legs rebel. Even if your powers of concentration are exceptional, it's nearly impossible to run aggressively for 26.2 miles. By staying relaxed early in the race, you'll save more of your mental determination for the latter stages and will maintain a more even pace.

If a 5K or 10K goes poorly, you can run another a week or two later. When a marathon doesn't go as planned, however, it's usually months before you're ready to toe the starting line again. For this reason, the marathon may grow larger than life in your mind. You can keep the race in perspective by focusing on the essentials of the task. Find positive reinforcement in your training and other elements of preparation. Focusing on your strengths builds confidence and peace of mind. By knowing that you systematically prepared for the race, you'll be able to relax and further increase your odds of marathon success.

Marathon Training Schedule
Schedule A: Less than 40 miles/week

Weeks to goal	LR1	LR2	Lactate-threshold workouts	$\dot{V}O_2max$ workouts	Basic speed	Week's mileage
17	11	7	—	—	—	25
16	12	7	—	—	8 × 100 meters	26
15	13	8	2 × 1 1/2-mile LT intervals	—	—	27
14	13	8	2 × 1 3/4-mile LT intervals	—	—	28
13	14	8	—	4 × 1K at 8K-10K race pace	—	29
12	15	9	2 × 2-mile LT intervals	—	—	31
11	16	9	—	4 × 1,200 meters at 8K-10K race pace	—	32
10	14	10	3-mile tempo run	—	—	32
9	17	10	4-mile tempo run	—	—	34
8	18	11	—	—	10 × 100 meters	34

Marathon Training Schedule
Schedule A: Less than 40 miles/week

Weeks to goal	LR1	LR2	Lactate-threshold workouts	$\dot{V}O_2$max workouts	Basic speed	Week's mileage
7	14	11	5-mile tempo run	–	–	35
6	19	10	–	–	10 × 100 meters	36
5	14	11	6-mile tempo run	–	–	37
4	20	10	–	–	10 × 100 meters	40
3	17	10	8K to 15K tune-up race	–	8 × 100 meters	38

Three-Week Taper

Weeks to goal	Mon	Tues	Wed	Thu	Fri	Sat	Sun	Mile-age
2	Off	4 miles	5 miles with 8 × 100 meters	3 miles	4-mile tempo run	Off	14 miles	33
1	Off	3 miles	3 × 1 mile at 10K race pace	Off	5 miles	Off	11 miles	26
Race Week	Off	4 miles	6 miles with 2-mile de-pletion run	3 miles	Off	3 miles	**Goal race**	16 (up to race day)

Marathon Training Schedule
Schedule B: 40–60 miles/week

Weeks to goal	LR1	LR2	Lactate-threshold workouts	$\dot{V}O_2$max workouts	Basic speed	Week's mileage
17	13	8	–	–	–	45
16	14	8	–	–	10 × 100 meters	46
15	15	9	2 × 1 1/2-mile LT intervals	–	–	47
14	15	9	2 × 1 3/4-mile LT intervals	–	–	48
13	16	10	–	5 × 1K at 8K-10K race pace	–	49
12	17	10	2 × 2-mile LT intervals	–	–	50
11	18	10	–	5 × 1,200 meters at 8K-10K race pace	–	51
10	18	10	4-mile tempo run	–	–	52
9	16	11	5-mile tempo run	–	–	50
8	20	11	–	–	12 × 100 meters	54

Marathon Training Schedule
Schedule B: 40–60 miles/week

Weeks to goal	LR1	LR2	Lactate-threshold workouts	$\dot{V}O_2$max workouts	Basic speed	Week's mileage
7	15	12	6-mile tempo run	–	–	52
6	21	11	–	–	12 × 100 meters	56
5	15	13	8K to 15K tune-up race	–	12 × 100 meters	56
4	20	13	–	5× 1K at 5K race pace	–	60
3	17	12	8K to 15K tune-up race	–	12 × 100 meters	56

Three-Week Taper

Weeks to goal	Mon	Tues	Wed	Thu	Fri	Sat	Sun	Mileage
2	Off	5 miles	9 miles with 10 × 100 meters	5 miles	5-mile tempo run	5 miles	16 miles	49
1	Off	6 miles	3 × 1 mile at 10K race pace	6 miles	Off	5 miles	12 miles	37
Race Week	Off	5 miles	7 miles with 2 1/2-mile depletion run	5 miles	Off	3 miles	Goal race	20 (up to race day)

Marathon Training Schedule
Schedule C: More than 60 miles/week

Weeks to goal	LR1	LR2	Lactate-threshold workouts	$\dot{V}O_2max$ workouts	Basic speed	Week's mileage	Per-centage of peak
17	15	10	–	–	–	60	70
16	16	11	–	–	10 × 100 meters	63	74
15	17	11	2 × 1 1/2-mile LT intervals	–	–	66	78
14	15	11	2 × 1 3/4-mile LT intervals	–	–	68	80
13	18	12	–	6 × 1K at 8K-10K race pace	–	70	82
12	15	12	2 × 2-mile LT intervals	–	–	70	82
11	19	12	–	6 × 1,200 meters at 8K-10K race pace	–	74	87
10	16	13	4-mile tempo run	–	–	66	78
9	20	13	5-mile tempo run	–	–	78	92
8	17	13	–	–	12 × 100 meters	78	92

Marathon Training Schedule
Schedule C: More than 60 miles/week

Weeks to goal	LR1	LR2	Lactate-threshold workouts	$\dot{V}O_2$max workouts	Basic speed	Week's mileage	Per-centage of peak
7	21	14	6-mile tempo run	–	–	82	96
6	17	14	Last 2 miles of LR2	–	12 × 100 meters	78	92
5	22	14	–	–	12 × 100 meters	85	100
4	15	12	8K to 15K tune-up race	5 × 600 meters at 5K race pace	–	76	89
3	20	14	–	–	12 × 100 meters	76	89

Three-Week Taper							
Weeks to goal	Mon	Tues	Wed	Thu	Fri	Sat	Sun	Mile-age
2	6 miles	7 miles	11 miles with 12 × 100 meters	8 miles	5 miles	8K to 15K tune-up race	17 miles	66
1	Off	6 miles	3 × 1 mile at 10K race pace	9 miles	6 miles	6 miles	13 miles	49
Race Week	5 miles	5 miles	8 miles with 3-mile de-pletion run	5 miles	Off	4 miles	Goal race	27 (up to race day)

CHAPTER 10

Training to Race
Cross-Country

© Victah

This chapter focuses on cross-country, the most natural and, to many, the most enjoyable, form of long-distance running. Cross-country racing is both gut wrenching and exhilarating. It requires top-notch cardiovascular fitness as well as the ability to run well on challenging courses—up and down hills and over various types of terrain.

Physiology of Cross-Country Races

Physiologically, cross-country races require a high $\dot{V}O_2$max and a high lactate threshold. Cross-country races of about 5K in length emphasize high $\dot{V}O_2$max more than high lactate threshold, while races of 8K to 12K put roughly equal emphasis on these two physiological attributes. Cross-country also requires the less quantifiable skills of being able to run strongly up and down hills and on various surfaces. This makes cross-country running unique. With the right balance of training, your body will adapt and improve in all these areas.

As discussed in chapter 2, your $\dot{V}O_2$max is determined partly by genetics and partly by training. You can improve your $\dot{V}O_2$max by including specific sessions in your program to stimulate this adaptation. The ability to improve in cross-country also requires a high lactate threshold, which means that lactate doesn't start to accumulate in your muscles and blood until you reach a high percentage of your $\dot{V}O_2$max. You can increase the percentage of your $\dot{V}O_2$max at which your lactate threshold occurs by designing your training specifically to stimulate this adaptation. With a properly designed schedule, you can increase your lactate threshold for many years.

The training schedules in this chapter improve your $\dot{V}O_2$max and lactate threshold, and thereby improve your cross-country performance. The schedules also emphasize running on the types of terrain and surfaces that you'll encounter in your races. This acclimation will be invaluable when it's time to toe the starting line.

Setting Goals

Setting goals for cross-country differs from setting goals for track or road races because times in cross-country are relatively meaningless. Because of differences among courses, you could run a better race, but a slower time, on a course that's wet and muddy or has more hills. If you run several races on the same course, you can gauge your progress by your times. If you're racing on different courses,

Lynn Jennings

© Victah

10K Personal Record: 31:19
Career highlight at distance: 1st, 1990-92 World Cross-Country Championships
Training and racing emphasis: Lynn Jennings is one of the most successful women in American distance-running history. She owes part of that success to a well-rounded program that emphasizes a few peak performances each year, with other races used as stepping stones to her most important goals. For years, she has used cross-country training and racing not only as one of her focuses but also as important preparation for summer road and track racing.

Jennings hasn't contested the late-March world cross-country championships in recent years, but she still keys on the US national championships in late November or early December, an event that she has won a record nine times. Her fall cross-country season usually follows a varied spring road-race schedule, in which she mixes distances between 5K and 15K. During the summer, she usually focuses on track races, using races as short as 1500m to prepare her for major championships at 5,000m and 10,000m. About having a distinct cross-country season, she says, "It's a nice change of pace. The forgiving surfaces are very beneficial; they save my legs. The proof of that is that I don't have any chronic overuse injuries."

Jennings is known for being methodical in her preparations. When building toward the national cross-country championships, she trains similarly to the way she does when getting ready for long track races—an appropriate blend of $\dot{V}O_2$max and lactate-threshold workouts, while not neglecting her endurance and leg turnover work. One big difference is that, rather than the track, she does her hard workouts

→

on footing similar to that she'll face in cross-country races. "I have three different venues with different footings," she says about her cross-country-specific training. "The workouts don't really differ much from track workouts, except that time becomes relatively unimportant in and of itself. Still, my coach, John Babington, times my intervals, so there is a comparative feature—if I run the same loop and run 5:10, 5:08, 5:20, then I know I'm off." On her recovery days during cross-country season, Jennings makes more of an effort than during the rest of the year to run on trails to further condition her legs for cross-country's uneven footing.

however, you can measure your performance only by comparing it to the performance of other runners. Fortunately, this is often possible because the same runners tend to show up at cross-country races.

Training for Cross-Country

This chapter includes four schedules—two schedules for runners training for races of 3K to 7K (1.9 to 4.2 miles) and two schedules for races of 8K to 12K (4.9 to 7.4 miles). The schedules will prepare you for the unique demands of cross-country racing. To race consistently well in cross-country, you must be ready for uphills, downhills, mud, rocks, and other obstacles. You'll beat equally talented runners if you gear your training to simulate race conditions. By training on hills, soft surfaces, and uneven terrain, you'll prepare your muscles and cardiovascular system to deal with cross-country conditions. Each year, several relatively unknown men and women use this strategy to beat better known track and road racers for spots on the U.S. team that competes at the world cross-country championships.

The cross-country schedules were developed according to the priorities shown in tables 10.1 and 10.2. Among the four types of training discussed in chapters 2 and 3, lactate-threshold training and $\dot{V}O_2$max training are most important for cross-country, followed by pure endurance training and then basic speed. The schedules assume that you're starting with a basic level of fitness. Before the start of the schedule, several months before your goal race, you should work on building endurance; pure endurance training should be your highest priority during that time. The base training schedules in chapter 4 will prepare you to start the cross-country schedules. During the 12 weeks, the top priority in the schedules gradually shifts from lactate-threshold training toward $\dot{V}O_2$max training.

10.1 **Training Priorities for 3K to 7K Cross-Country, in Order of Importance During the Schedule**			
	Preschedule	First 6 weeks	Last 6 weeks
Basic speed	4	4	4
$\dot{V}O_2$max	3	1	1
Lactate threshold	2	2	2
Pure endurance	1	3	3

10.2 **Training Priorities for 8K to 12K Cross-Country, in Order of Importance During the Schedule**			
	Preschedule	First 6 weeks	Last 6 weeks
Basic speed	4	4	4
$\dot{V}O_2$max	3	2	1
Lactate threshold	2	1	2
Pure endurance	1	3	3

Schedules Explained

The 12-week training schedules are long enough to provide a strong stimulus to improve performance but short enough to keep you focused on your goal race. The schedules are organized vertically by the number of weeks until the race, so that your goal race is always your reference point. By looking down any of the columns, you can easily see how the workouts progress during the 12 weeks for that type of training.

The schedules are also organized horizontally, so that you can quickly view the key workouts for the week. In this way, it's easy to see which training stimuli are emphasized that week and that you don't have to do too much in any week. The schedules don't specify which days of the week to do the workouts; that depends on the schedule that organizes the rest of your life.

Longest run   The schedules gradually increase your long runs to help prepare you for the pure endurance component of cross-country. The distance of the longest run in the schedules varies, from 9 miles for a 3K to 7K racer training less than 35 miles per week, to 14 miles for an 8K to 12K racer training more than 45 miles per week. Nonetheless, the principle is the same—long runs aren't jogs. To stimulate desirable physiological adaptations, such as increased capillary density, do your long runs 1:30 to 2:30 per mile slower than your 5K race pace or 1:15 to 2:15 per mile slower than your 8K to 10K race pace.

Second longest run   The purpose of the second longest run for the week is to reinforce the training adaptations of the long runs. Try to do these workouts over similar terrain and surfaces to the courses for your cross-country races. If your races will have hills, then be sure to include some in your training runs. By training off the road, you'll build muscular endurance in your calf muscles, which will help you maintain a faster pace during your cross-country races. Runners who train primarily on the roads often find that their calf muscles fatigue quickly during cross-country races because those muscles work much harder on soft surfaces.

Lactate-threshold workouts   The workouts in this column include tempo runs, LT intervals, LT hills, time trials, and tune-up races. Tempo runs, LT intervals, and LT hills were explained in detail in chapter 3. Tempo runs are continuous runs of 20 to 40 minutes at lactate-threshold pace. Lactate-threshold pace is approximately your 15K to half-marathon race pace. (For other ways to estimate lactate-threshold pace, see chapter 3.) For these workouts, warm up for about two miles, run the tempo run at lactate-threshold pace, and then cool down for a mile or two. Run LT intervals at the same pace as tempo runs but instead of one continuous run, break up the distance into two to four segments, with several minutes of slow running after each. In an LT hill workout, you run a course containing several long, challenging hills and work the hills at lactate-threshold intensity. If possible, do your LT workouts for cross-country off-road.

   Time trials and tune-up races are more intense than the other types of lactate-threshold workouts. Time trials are useful as a way of gauging your training progress. By running hard on a cross-country course that you've run before, you can get an indication of your comparative level of fitness. Tune-up races are competitions that you enter as preparation for your goal race.

   During the 12 weeks, the lactate-threshold workouts progress from LT intervals and LT hills to tempo runs to a time trial and tune-

Paul Koech

© Victah

10K Personal Record: 26:36
Career highlight at distance: 2nd, 1998 World Cross Country Championships

Training and racing emphasis: Paul Koech follows a program that has become common—and incredibly successful—for top-flight nonmarathoners from Kenya. After resting for a few weeks in the fall, he begins cross-country training in November, with no run exceeding 90 minutes. After four weeks of base training, he begins to run tune-up cross-country races in December and January in Europe, then returns to Kenya. There, in the group training camps that have become legendary, he trains three times a day, pointing toward the Kenyan Armed Forces championships, then the national championships, and culminating in the world championships at the end of March. In 1998, he placed second in the senior men's 12K race there, which is generally considered the most competitive distance race in the world. Koech then runs a few road races in the US and Europe in April and May as a transition to his track season. During the summer, he races from 3,000m to 10,000m at the highest-quality track meets in the world. After track season is over, he runs a few road races in Europe before taking a break and starting the process anew. Following this program in 1997, he placed fourth in the world in cross-country and 10,000m on the track, ran the third-fastest track 10K in history, and in the fall ran a world best 44:45 for 10 miles.

As do many top Kenyans, Koech relies on a strong cross-country season as the anchor of his training and racing. "When one succeeds in a cross-country season, one does quite fine the rest of the year," he says. "When you can run well in cross-country, you can run easily the

→

rest of the year on any surface. Cross-country builds up the body in areas where it might not be so strong, and it gives you a lot of endurance. Running up and down hills gives the body strength, so when you get to the flats, you can run quite nicely without much problem." When preparing for cross-country, Koech does as much of his training as possible on soft surfaces. "To succeed in cross-country," he says, "you must prepare on soft ground. All of my hard training for cross-country is on grass and loose roads to teach the body to run well over uneven ground."

up race. This sequence builds to a close simulation of the demands of cross-country racing. Besides providing physiological benefits, these workouts prepare you mentally for racing.

$\dot{V}O_2$max Workouts   These workouts are intervals of 1+ to 5 minutes. For cross-country, you should run these workouts on a golf course, grass fields, trails, or other varied terrain. The length of the intervals, therefore, is measured in minutes rather than distance. Some of the $\dot{V}O_2$max sessions for cross-country training specify hill repeats. As discussed in chapter 2, the greatest stimulus to improving $\dot{V}O_2$max is to train at an intensity that requires 95 to 100 percent of your current $\dot{V}O_2$max. This corresponds to about your 3K to 5K race pace. The rest between intervals should be slow running that lasts 50 to 90 percent of the interval's duration. When you run intervals off the track, you can estimate the correct pace through perceived exertion or, if you wear a heart monitor, by running at the same heart rate that you reach when running at 3K to 5K race pace.

Fartlek training is a demanding yet enjoyable form of $\dot{V}O_2$max workout for cross-country training. Fartlek (Swedish for speed play) consists of alternating running at $\dot{V}O_2$max pace and slowing to recovery pace. These workouts need no structure—just accelerate and hold the pace as long as you can, then slow until you recover enough to be able to pick up the pace again. Overall, at least half of the duration of the workout should be at $\dot{V}O_2$max effort (not counting your warm-up and cool-down, which should be the same as for a $\dot{V}O_2$max workout on the track).

Basic speed   These workouts are accelerations up to full speed, with the objective of improving your leg turnover. For cross-country, you should run these sessions on grass. By doing these workouts you will be able to shift gears during the race and finish with a stronger kick.

Putting it all together   As an example of how to structure the week's training, look at eight weeks to go on Schedule A-2 (more than 35 miles per week in preparation for 3K to 7K cross-country races). The schedule for that week includes three workouts. Add easy recovery runs or cross-training as necessary to reach the total of 43 miles for the week (see table 10.3). For how to equate cross-training with running mileage, see chapter 4.

A typical way to complete this week's training is to do the longest run on Sunday, then run an easy 5 miles on Monday. Tuesday could be another recovery day consisting of an easy 6 miles. Wednesday would be time for a hard session, such as the fartlek run, representing a total of 8 miles with the warm-up and cool-down. Thursday's run could be the second longest run, followed by a rest day on Friday and an easy 6-miler on Saturday. You would complete the 43 miles in six days of running, with the workouts evenly spaced throughout the week. Do as much of your training as possible off-road to prepare specifically for cross-country.

Avoid doing important workouts on consecutive days. If you have to do most of your hard running on the weekends, recover from the two hard days with two easy days.

If you miss an important workout, don't try to make it up. If injury, fatigue, bad weather, or demands from the rest of your life put you behind schedule early in the week, don't run several hard sessions in a row to make up for lost time. If you try to squeeze several hard

Table 10.3	Properly Structuring a Sample Week From Cross-Country Schedule A-2
Sunday	10 miles
Monday	5 miles
Tuesday	6 miles
Wednesday	$\dot{V}O_2$max workout (8 miles, including warm-up, 25 minutes of fartlek, and cool-down)
Thursday	8 miles
Friday	Off
Saturday	6 miles
Mileage for week	43

sessions together, the quality of your workouts will go down and you'll increase your risk of injury. Instead, use the priorities outlined in tables 10.1 and 10.2 to determine the most important sessions for where you are in the schedule. For example, say you're following Schedule B-1, and with five weeks to go before your goal race, you can fit in only two important workouts. According to table 10.2, your top training priorities among the workouts scheduled for that week are VO_2max, building lactate threshold, and endurance, respectively. You'll note on Schedule B-1 for that week (see page 180) there is no VO_2max workout scheduled, but there is both a lactate-threshold and an endurance workout. Therefore, you would do the 3 × 7:00 at LT pace session listed as the week's lactate-threshold workout on one day and the 12-miler listed as the week's longest run on another day.

Runners following Schedules A-2 and B-2 who want to do more than the weekly mileage listed in the schedule should follow the trend in mileage outlined and simply adjust their mileage upward as a percentage of the prescribed mileage. Say that you're following Schedule B-2 and want to reach a peak mileage of 70 per week; this would occur with five weeks to go. As noted in Schedule B-2, with one week to go, you should be at roughly 80 percent of your peak, or 56 miles (70 × 80 percent). Follow this principle throughout the program. Build your mileage in the first part of the schedule, then taper as you approach your goal race.

Racing Strategy and Mental Approach

Cross-country racing tests your heart and soul. Unlike road racing, in which you tend to find a pace that you can hold for much of the race, in cross-country the pace and effort vary constantly. At times during the race you will think you can't hold on any longer, but then you'll reach a downhill and recover enough to hang on some more. You must be ready for the pace to vary depending on the footing and the terrain. If you are accustomed to racing on the roads or track, you may find cross-country mentally trying because you often don't get split times or see mile markers along the way, making it that much harder to dole out your effort intelligently.

In cross-country, the best place to make a move to beat another runner is on an uphill. The key is to run just off the other runner's shoulder, then pick up the pace to the top of the hill. The other runner generally tries to stay with you and assumes that you'll ease back slightly at the top. You should continue your surge for 100 meters or so past the crest. This tactic should allow you to open up a gap on the other runner and put enough distance between the two of you that he loses contact.

Never make a weak move. That only wastes energy, and your opponent gains confidence by easily covering your move. Also, never look back to see where someone is. When you look back, you give the runners behind you a psychological boost by letting them know that you're tired and worried about them. (You are, of course, but keep that to yourself.)

Cross-Country Races of 3K to 7K
Schedule A-1: Less than 35 miles/week

Weeks to goal	LR1	LR2	Lactate-threshold workouts	$\dot{V}O_2max$ workouts	Basic speed	Week's mileage
11		6	5 workout	LR2 is LT hill	— 8 × 0:20	23
10	7	5	—	16:00 fartlek	—	25
9	7	5	2 × 6:00 LT intervals	—	8 × 0:20	27
8	7	6	—	20:00 fartlek	—	29
7	8	6	2 × 7:00 LT intervals	—	8 × 0:20	31
6	8	6	—	5 × 2:00 rolling hills	—	33
5	9	7	3 × 6:00 LT intervals	—	8 × 0:20	35
4	8	6	—	3 × 3:00 hill loop	—	33
3	8	6	—	2 × 2:00, steady 10:00, 2 × 2:00	—	31
2	7	5	Cross-country tune-up race	—	8 × 0:45	29
1	6	5	—	6 × 1:30 rolling hills	8 × 0:20	27
Race week	5	4	**Goal race**	—	8 × 0:20	21

Cross-Country Races of 3K to 7K
Schedule A-2: More than 35 miles/week

Weeks to goal	LR1	LR2	Lactate-threshold workouts	$\dot{V}O_2$max workouts	Basic speed	Week's mileage	Percentage of peak
11	9	7	LR2 is LT hill workout	–	10 × 0:30	35	70
10	10	7	LR2 is LT hill workout	20:00 fartlek	–	38	76
9	10	7	2 × 6:00 LT intervals	–	10 × 0:30	40	80
8	10	8	–	25:00 fartlek	–	43	86
7	11	8	2 × 7:00 LT intervals	–	10 × 0:30	46	92
6	11	8	–	5 × 2:30 rolling hills	–	48	96
5	12	9	3 × 6:00 LT intervals	–	10 × 0:30	50	100
4	11	8	–	4 × 3:00 hill loop	–	48	96
3	11	8	–	3 × 2:00, steady 10:00, 3 × 2:00	–	46	92
2	10	7	Cross-country tune-up race	–	10 × 0:30	44	88
1	9	7	–	6 × 1:30 rolling hills	10 × 0:30	42	84
Race week	7	6	**Goal race**	–	6 × 0:45	36	72

Cross-Country Races of 8K to 12K
Schedule B-1: Less than 45 miles/week

Weeks to goal	LR1	LR2	Lactate-threshold workouts	$\dot{V}O_2$max workouts	Basic speed	Week's mileage
11	9	8	LR2 is LT hill workout	–	10 × 0:30	35
10	9	8	–	25:00 fartlek	–	37
9	10	8	2 × 7:00 LT intervals	–	10 × 0:30	39
8	10	9	–	30:00 fartlek	–	41
7	11	9	2 × 8:00 LT intervals	–	10 × 0:30	43
6	11	9	–	3 × 4:00 hill loop	–	45
5	12	10	3 × 7:00 LT intervals	–	10 × 0:30	45
4	12	10	–	4 × 4:00 hill loop	–	43
3	11	9	–	3 × 3:00, steady 15:00, 3 × 3:00	–	41
2	10	8	Cross-country tune-up race	–	8 × 0:45	39
1	9	7	–	8 × 1:30 rolling hills	10 × 0:30	37
Race week	7	5	**Goal race**	–	6 × 0:45	35

Cross-Country Races of 8K to 12K
Schedule B-2: More than 45 miles/week

Weeks to goal	LR1	LR2	Lactate-threshold workouts	$\dot{V}O_2$max workouts	Basic speed	Week's mileage	Per-centage of peak
11	10	8	LR2 is LT hill workout	–	10 × 0:30	45	75
10	11	8	LR2 is LT hill workout	30:00 fartlek	–	48	80
9	11	8	2 × 8:00 LT intervals	–	10 × 0:30	50	83
8	12	9	–	35:00 fartlek	–	53	88
7	12	9	3 × 6:00 LT intervals	–	10 × 0:30	55	92
6	13	9	–	4 × 4:00 hill loops	–	57	95
5	14	10	3 × 8:00 LT intervals	–	10 × 0:30	60	100
4	13	10	–	5 × 4:00 hill loop	–	55	92
3	12	9	–	3 × 3:00, steady 15:00, 3 × 3:00	–	52	87
2	11	8	Cross-country tune-up race	–	10 × 0:30	50	83
1	9	7	–	8 × 1:30 rolling hills	10 × 0:30	47	78
Race week	7	5	**Goal race**	–	10 × 0:30	45	75

Appendix A: Equivalent Times for 5K Through Marathon

5K	8K	10K	15K	10 miles	20K	Half marathon	Marathon
13:00	21:36	27:12	42:04	45:46	57:31	1:01:02	2:09:21
14:00	23:16	29:17	45:18	49:18	1:01:57	1:05:44	2:19:18
15:00	24:55	31:23	48:32	52:49	1:06:22	1:10:25	2:29:15
16:00	26:35	33:28	51:47	56:21	1:10:54	1:15:07	2:39:12
17:00	28:15	35:33	55:01	59:51	1:15:13	1:19:48	2:49:09
18:00	29:54	37:39	58:15	1:03:23	1:19:39	1:24:30	2:59:06
19:00	31:34	39:45	1:01:29	1:06:54	1:24:04	1:29:12	3:09:03
20:00	33:13	41:50	1:04:43	1:10:25	1:28:30	1:33:54	3:19:00
21:00	34:53	43:56	1:07:57	1:13:56	1:32:55	1:38:35	3:28:57
22:00	36:32	46:02	1:11:12	1:17:27	1:37:21	1:43:17	3:38:54
23:00	38:12	48:07	1:14:26	1:20:59	1:41:46	1:47:59	3:48:51
24:00	39:52	50:12	1:17:46	1:24:30	1:46:12	1:52:40	3:58:48

Appendix B: Pace Chart for 400 Meters to Marathon

400M	600M	800M	1,000M	1,200M	1,600M	3K	5K
56	84	1:52	2:20	2:48	3:44		
58	87	1:56	2:25	2:54	3:52		
60	90	2:00	2:30	3:00	4:00	7:30	
62	93	2:04	2:35	3:06	4:08	7:45	12:55
64	96	2:08	2:40	3:12	4:16	8:00	13:20
66	99	2:12	2:45	3:18	4:24	8:15	13:45
68	1:42	2:16	2:50	3:24	4:32	8:30	14:10
70	1:45	2:20	2:55	3:30	4:40	8:45	14:35
72	1:48	2:24	3:00	3:36	4:48	9:00	15:00
74	1:51	2:28	3:05	3:42	4:56	9:15	15:25
76	1:54	2:32	3:10	3:48	5:04	9:30	15:50
78	1:57	2:36	3:15	3:54	5:12	9:45	16:15
80	2:00	2:40	3:20	4:00	5:20	10:00	16:40
82	2:03	2:44	3:25	4:06	5:28	10:15	17:05
84	2:06	2:48	3:30	4:12	5:36	10:30	17:30
86	2:09	2:52	3:35	4:18	5:44	10:45	17:55
88	2:12	2:56	3:40	4:24	5:52	11:00	18:20
90	2:15	3:00	3:45	4:30	6:00	11:15	18:45
92	2:18	3:04	3:50	4:36	6:08	11:30	19:10
94	2:21	3:08	3:55	4:42	6:16	11:45	19:35
96	2:24	3:12	4:00	4:48	6:24	12:00	20:00
98	2:27	3:16	4:05	4:54	6:32	12:15	20:25
1:40	2:30	3:20	4:10	5:00	6:40	12:30	20:50
1:42	2:33	3:24	4:15	5:06	6:48	12:45	21:15
1:44	2:36	3:28	4:20	5:12	6:56	13:00	21:40
1:46	2:39	3:32	4:25	5:18	7:04	13:15	22:05
1:48	2:42	3:36	4:30	5:24	7:12	13:30	22:30
1:50	2:45	3:40	4:35	5:30	7:20	13:45	22:55
1:52	2:48	3:44	4:40	5:36	7:28	14:00	23:20
1:54	2:51	3:48	4:45	5:42	7:36	14:15	23:45
1:56	2:54	3:52	4:50	5:48	7:44	14:30	24:10
1:58	2:57	3:56	4:55	5:54	7:52	14:45	24:35
2:00	3:00	4:00	5:00	6:00	8:00	15:00	25:00
2:02	3:03	4:04	5:05	6:06	8:08	15:15	25:25
2:04	3:06	4:08	5:10	6:12	8:16	15:30	25:50
2:06	3:09	4:12	5:15	6:18	8:24	15:45	26:15
2:08	3:12	4:16	5:20	6:24	8:32	16:00	26:40
2:10	3:15	4:20	5:25	6:30	8:40	16:15	27:05
2:12	3:18	4:24	5:30	6:36	8:48	16:30	27:30
2:14	3:21	4:28	5:35	6:42	8:56	16:45	27:55
2:16	3:24	4:32	5:40	6:48	9:04	17:00	28:20